The Uncor

MW00655669

In *The Unconscious: A Contemporary Introduction*, Joseph Newirth presents a critical and comparative analysis of the unconscious and its evolution from a positivist to a postmodern frame of reference.

This book presents five theories, each of which offers different and important conceptualizations of the unconscious, and each of which contains a rich palate of ideas through which to approach clinical work. These psychoanalytic theories are thought of as spokes on a wheel emanating from the center of Freud's concept of the unconscious. In addition to presenting Freud's development of the unconscious, Newirth includes discussions of interpersonal/relational psychoanalysis; developmental approaches to the unconscious, including Kohut, Winnicott, and Fonagy; Kleinian approaches to the unconscious; and linguistic theories of the unconscious, including Matte Blanco and Lacan. The last chapter illustrates the use of contemporary psychoanalytic concepts in the clinical work with a contemporary patient. The book encourages a comparative view of psychoanalytic theory and technique and aims to move to a more useful, generalizable concept of the unconscious for the contemporary patient.

This book will be of great interest to psychoanalysts, psychologists, and anyone interested in the evolution and application of the unconscious as a concept.

Joseph Newirth is Professor Emeritus at the Gordon F. Derner School of Psychology, Adelphi University, USA. He is on the faculty of several psychoanalytic institutes and was the Director of the Postdoctoral Program in Psychoanalysis at Adelphi University. His previous books received the Gradiva Prize (2004) and the American Board and Academy of Psychoanalysis Book Prize (2019). He is currently in practice in New York City.

Routledge Introductions to Contemporary Psychoanalysis

Series Editor
Aner Govrin, Ph.D.

Executive Editor
Yael Peri Herzovich

"Routledge Introductions to Contemporary Psychoanalysis" is one of the prominent psychoanalytic publishing ventures of our day. It will comprise dozens of books that will serve as concise introductions dedicated to influential concepts, theories, leading figures, and techniques in psychoanalysis covering every important aspect of psychoanalysis.

The length of each book is fixed at 40,000 words.

The series' books are designed to be easily accessible to provide informative answers in various areas of psychoanalytic thought. Each book will provide updated ideas on topics relevant to contemporary psychoanalysis – from the unconscious and dreams, projective identification and eating disorders, through neuropsychoanalysis, colonialism, and spiritual-sensitive psychoanalysis. Books will also be dedicated to prominent figures in the field, such as Melanie Klein, Jaque Lacan, Sandor Ferenczi, Otto Kernberg, and Michael Eigen.

Not serving solely as an introduction for beginners, the purpose of the series is to offer compendiums of information on particular topics within different psychoanalytic schools. We ask authors to review a topic but also address the readers with their own personal views and contribution to the specific chosen field. Books will make intricate ideas comprehensible without compromising their complexity.

We aim to make contemporary psychoanalysis more accessible to both clinicians and the general educated public.

Aner Govrin
Editor

Christopher Bollas: A Contemporary Introduction
Steve Jaron

Eating Disorders: A Contemporary Introduction
Tom Wooldridge

Michael Eigen: A Contemporary Introduction
Loray Daws

Psychoanalytic Field Theory: A Contemporary Introduction
Giuseppe Civitarese

Psychoanalysis and Colonialism: A Contemporary Introduction
Sally Swartz

W.R. Bion's Theories of Mind: A Contemporary Introduction
Annie Reiner

Herbert Rosenfeld: A Contemporary Introduction
Robert Hinshelwood

Neuropsychoanalysis: A Contemporary Introduction
Georg Northoff

Spiritually-Sensitive Psychoanalysis: A Contemporary Introduction
Gideon Lev

Psychoanalysis and Homosexuality: A Contemporary Introduction
Leezah Hertzmann and Juliet Newbigin

Melanie Klein: A Contemporary Introduction
Penelope Garvey

The Unconscious: A Contemporary Introduction
Joseph Newirth

Guilt: A Contemporary Introduction
Donald L. Carveth

I dedicate this book to my family: Eleanor, Mike, Karen, Tyler, Hazel, and Violet. You have been a constant source of love, support, and energy throughout this project, and I could not imagine doing this without your company.

The Unconscious

A Contemporary Introduction

Joseph Newirth

Routledge
Taylor & Francis Group

LONDON AND NEW YORK

Designed cover image: © Michal Heiman, Asylum 1855–2020, The Sleeper (video, psychoanalytic sofa and Plate 34), exhibition view, Herzliya Museum of Contemporary Art, 2017.

First published 2023
by Routledge
4 Park Square, Milton Park, Abingdon, Oxon OX14 4RN

and by Routledge
605 Third Avenue, New York, NY 10158

Routledge is an imprint of the Taylor & Francis Group, an informa business

© 2023 Joseph Newirth

The right of Joseph Newirth to be identified as author of this work has been asserted in accordance with sections 77 and 78 of the Copyright, Designs and Patents Act 1988.

All rights reserved. No part of this book may be reprinted or reproduced or utilised in any form or by any electronic, mechanical, or other means, now known or hereafter invented, including photocopying and recording, or in any information storage or retrieval system, without permission in writing from the publishers.

Trademark notice: Product or corporate names may be trademarks or registered trademarks, and are used only for identification and explanation without intent to infringe.

British Library Cataloguing-in-Publication Data
A catalogue record for this book is available from the British Library

ISBN: 978-0-367-52516-3 (hbk)
ISBN: 978-0-367-52517-0 (pbk)
ISBN: 978-1-003-05827-4 (ebk)

DOI: 10.4324/9781003058274

Typeset in Times New Roman
by Taylor & Francis Books

Contents

Acknowledgments

I want to express my deepest gratitude to Aner Govrin and Tair Caspi, the editors of this series at Routledge, for their enthusiasm and support during this project. I also want to thank my colleagues at the Derner School of Psychology, New York University, the National Training Program (NTP), and National Institute for the Psychotherapies (NIP) for their interest and support of my ongoing interest in the unconscious. I want to thank my students and supervisees at Derner and the NTP and those who I have consulted with independent of these institutions for supporting my growth through asking provocative and stimulating questions and being free enough to expose their vulnerabilities, along with accepting my parallel experiences of confusion and doubt in our work as psychoanalysts and psychotherapists. I want to thank my colleagues and friends for their interest in and support of my ideas about psychoanalysis: Richard Billow, Karen Lombardi, Robert Schwalbe, Robert Shapiro, Margret Black, Susan Jaffe, Joyce Selter, Stephanie Lewin, Heidi Kling, and Michael Garfinkle. Most importantly, I want to thank my patients for trusting me and allowing me to accompany them on their journeys of self-discovery and growth, often finding ourselves in the depths and heights of human experience. Each of you has been an extremely valuable companion on this ongoing project of expanding our understanding of the unconscious.

Thanks!

Introduction

You Are Not the Master in Your Own House

Introduction

Sigmund Freud (Bloom, 1985) was one of the most influential voices of our time, changing our view on the nature of being human and arguing that we are not masters in our own house, that our motives are outside of awareness, unconscious. There are few people unfamiliar with Freud and the core concept of psychoanalysis, the unconscious, representing hidden or shameful motives, unacceptable thoughts, unbidden actions, and experiences of guilt. However, Freud did not discover the unconscious; it has always been a part of common folk knowledge. In earlier times, unconscious experiences were disowned, attributed to a mysterious other, seen as demonic possession or fate, expressed in the biblical expression "the sins of the fathers are visited on the children." Freud would have thought of these historic references to disowned action (Schafer, 1976), 'not me' experiences, as expressions of unconscious wishes, thoughts, and motives which were split off from conscious awareness and personal responsibility (Newirth, 2003). Freud's development of psychoanalysis and the concept of the unconscious was a revolutionary moment in the history of knowledge, making the mysteries of being human a subject to be studied and understood; bringing a scientific perspective to what had primarily existed as folk knowledge. Freud's many biographers have highlighted his personal and professional journey; in this book, I want to focus on the evolution of the concept of the unconscious and its operational twin, the psychoanalytic method,

DOI: 10.4324/9781003058274-1

which Freud developed simultaneously with his evolving theory of mental structure. In this book, I highlight how Freud's and others' theoretical concept of the unconscious was an outgrowth of work with patients, the clinical method, which became an algorithm for understanding unconscious phenomena and a procedure for psychoanalytic therapy; for making the unconscious conscious, creating the conditions for symptom relief and transforming neurotic misery into normal misery (Freud, 1893–1895).

All psychoanalytic theories differentiate concepts of unconscious and conscious organizations of experience[1] which reflect and define that theory's method of therapy, its understanding of psychopathology, psychological health, and the possibilities of growth. As an evolving and living field, psychoanalysis has had many contributors who have reworked Freud's concepts while maintaining an absolute belief in the importance of the unconscious as the critical structure of the mind. Although evolution seems to be a convenient way to consider the expanding field of psychoanalytic theory and practice, this view suggests a more linear line of development than we actually see. A better model for understanding the multiple concepts of the unconscious within contemporary psychoanalysis may be a wheel, with Freud's seminal contributions at the center and each post-Freudian contribution existing as a spoke coming from the center, expanding and elaborating a particular set of ideas in relation to other contemporary ideas emerging within a particular cultural zeitgeist.

All psychoanalytic theories have a primary belief in the centrality of the unconscious as the source of an analysand's difficulty and as an implicit structure which organizes the analyst's participation and interventions directed at engaging the patient's unconscious, facilitating structural change, symptom resolution, and growth. However, not all theories present an explicit description of the unconscious as a structure, as did Freud, and often we need to infer how the unconscious is conceptualized by viewing the analyst's interventions, participation in therapy, and understanding of the patient's dynamics.

Freud began his career working with hysterical patients who presented various symptoms often involving inhibitions, difficulties with memory, and odd repetitive movements and sounds. As a neurologist, he thought of these difficulties as reflecting forms of brain or neurological disorders and focused on finding the pathology within the patient, analogizing this early approach to psychological treatment to a surgeon draining an infection. Contemporary views of psychopathology, the unconscious, mental structure, and the psychoanalytic method have moved away from Freud's one-person biological perspective, developing two-person perspectives in which the individual's early experience and his/her cultural context determine many aspects of his/her unconscious. These contemporary psychoanalytic approaches have largely moved away from Freud's one-person, intrapsychic perspective, developing treatment paradigms focused on the "here and now" experiences between patient and analyst, in contrast to Freud's interpretive focus on remembering repressed wishes and events. I want to begin by describing Freud's development of the twin concepts of the unconscious and the clinical method of classical psychoanalysis and then move on to four post-Freudian approaches to the unconscious and the clinical method.

Overview

The first chapter presents a historic introduction to Freud's concept of the unconscious, describing how his experiences with patients led to the development of the concept of the unconscious, from a simple topographic or phenomenological model of conscious and unconscious experience to a more complex, dynamic model of the unconscious as an active force expressed in symptoms, resistance, and unhappy life choices. This discussion will emphasize the relationship between unconscious experience and clinical work, including dreams, slips of the tongue, humor, acting out, interpretation, constructions, and transference enactments.

Freud developed several dimensions of the unconscious which all psychoanalytic theories should consider in their conceptualization of the unconscious:

- The topographic model, which is a phenomenological approach describing the separation of conscious and unconscious experience.

- A structural model defining the relationship between conscious and unconscious experience and the interplay between the structures of the mind such as the id, ego, and superego.
- A developmental model including dynamic narratives such as the Oedipus myth, the libidinal stages of development, and the relationship between maternal and paternal behavior and the developing child.
- The nature of mental experience: memory, dreams, psychic and material reality, and how these inner processes represent and relate to present experience.
- A motivational theory describing concepts such as anxiety, sexuality, destructiveness, envy, and the pleasure principle.

The second chapter present the interpersonal, relational, and cultural psychoanalytic concepts of the unconscious which focus on anxiety as a social experience rather than an aspect of instinct or drive, The theories view parental disapproval as the main motivation which shapes the self as a system organized to avoid anxiety and maintain security and the consistency of experience. Rather than the unconscious being thought of as an inner structure, it becomes a system of avoidances, of not knowing, and the analytic process becomes organized as directed towards an expansion of awareness. As interpersonal theory evolved into relational psychoanalysis, the practice of psychotherapy moved from an expansion of the patient's awareness to an experiential emphasis on mutuality and symmetry within the transference–countertransference relationship and a potential dialogue in which both analyst and patient participate in creating new relationship models. Although interpersonal and relational psychoanalytic theories do not explicitly talk about the unconscious as a structure, they focus on the interplay between conscious and unconscious experience in both the analyst and patient, often focusing on concepts such as the unthought known (Stern, 2019) and the dialogue of the unconscious (Bass, 2015). The contributions of Mitchell, Aron, Bromberg, Davies, and Benjamin will be used to illustrate the implicit concept of the unconscious in relational psychoanalysis.

The third chapter presents developmental perspectives on the unconscious, focusing on the important contributions of Kohut,

Winnicott, and Fonagy. These theories argue for the necessity for a responsive maternal (parental) environment for the development of the unconscious, which is defined as the capacity to generate subjective meaning and engage in empathic intimate relationships. This group of theories reconceptualize the unconscious from the previous theories, which viewed the unconscious as a largely pathological, limiting organization of drives and anxiety focused on others' disapproval, into an organization underlying the capacity for growth, warmth, and meaningful relationships. These theories view the unconscious as developing through empathic attunement and transitional, playful relationships in which the individual is able to expand the meaningfulness of their lives. As in the previous chapter, these theorists present different terms for structural concepts of conscious and unconscious organizations of experience presenting models of potential growth and of stunted development. Developmental theorists present different forms of representation in unconscious and conscious experience. Many of these theorists implicitly emphasize the importance of pleasure and play as an aspect of growth and change. In this chapter, attachment theory and the work of the Boston Change Process Study Group will be used to illustrate similar perspectives on the unconscious as a developmental structure.

Chapter 4 presents the evolution of the Kleinian perspective, from her use of phantasy as an organizational concept replacing the biological concept of instinct through Bion's concept of the container contained, viewing the unconscious as the developing capacity to create meaning. In Kleinian theory, the central motivational process involves the mastery of aggression in the paranoid schizoid position which results in the development of the depressive position, reparation, and the capacity for symbolic thought and the ability to see others as separate, complex, whole people. This theory centers on the developing capacity for symbolization and making meaning. Bion's concept of thinking is a two-person process which extended Klein's concept of projective identification, emphasizing the importance of countertransference as a mode of therapeutic practice, a basic psychoanalytic tool similar to Freud's use of free association and free floating attention. The work of Grotstein, Ogden, Ferro, and other contemporary third-generation Kleinians will be emphasized as they describe how projective identification becomes the critical transformation process in the analytic relationship. These Kleinian theories conceptualize the unconscious as a developing intersubjective and intrasubjective structure for creating meaning.

Chapter 5 focuses on the influence of two theorists who are not usually presented together but who each developed theories which differentiate forms of representation, language, and thought which occur in conscious experience in the external world from that of unconscious experience of creating subjective meaning through metaphors and poetic or artistic creations. Both Matte Blanco and Lacan focused on the *Interpretation of Dreams* (Freud, 1900) as Freud's most significant text in which he presents the unconscious as a representational structure. Matte Blanco believes that conscious thought is based on asymmetrical logic in which we differentiate experience along the dimensions of time, place, person, and causality, while unconscious thought is based on symmetrical logic in which differences are effaced and similarities are developed. Lacan also focused on the *Interpretation of Dreams* (Freud, 1900), differentiating the importance of metaphor and language within the development of the unconscious. Lacan's emphasis on language is expressed in his metaphor that the "unconscious is structured like a language" (Dor, 1997). Lacan differentiated conscious and unconscious experience, focusing on three registers of comprehending and generating meaning: the imaginary, the symbolic, and the real. The imaginary register represents conscious organizations of experiencing oneself in a narcissistic state of oneness with the other, while the unconscious is formed by the child being introduced into the world of language, the law, and culture, which Lacan described as the symbolic register and which creates the possibility that the individual can know the rules (the law) of social being and know him/herself and the experience of desire. Like the theorists in the previous two chapters, both Lacan and Matte Blanco conceptualize the unconscious as a developmental process. Lacan conceives of the ego as a structure like Winnicott's false or objective self which conforms to the rules and demands of the other. For Lacan, the unconscious is a potential source of creative energy and also brings to bear acts of freedom, separating ourselves from the predetermined aspects of life that we were assigned to live as members of a family and cultural group.

The final chapter presents a contemporary patient who we might see as someone who does not know whether he is alive or dead. Our work in therapy focused on his developing capacity to feel, a sense of aliveness and an ability to utilize symbolic processes and self-reflective functioning. This chapter focuses on an inevitable lengthy period of deadness in work with these patients, the analyst's inability to think, projective identifications with patients' sense of deadness and failure, and the slow development of the container contained function. In this chapter, a view of the unconscious as a source of aliveness, a capacity to generate meaning, and a capacity to desire and develop relationships with others is presented.

In describing these different psychoanalytic perspectives of the unconscious, several themes emerge linking different versions of the concept of the unconscious. One major theme is that between phenomenological and structural views of the unconscious. Some theories emphasize one approach while minimizing the other, while others utilize both phenomenological and structural perspectives. These differences may be a function of the history of the psychoanalytic movement, how particular theories were formed as a reaction to earlier theories; some were reflections of the cultural period, the zeitgeist in which the theory developed, and some are a reflection of the personal preferences of the theorist and the adherents of those theories. It would seem that most contemporary practitioners develop their own mix of theoretical perspectives of the unconscious, reflecting and generating how they work with patients. In presenting this introduction to contemporary psychoanalytic theories, one factor that has been largely left out is how the psychoanalytic patient, the subject of analysis, has changed as a function of changes in our culture, the technological and socioeconomic developments which occurred from the early industrial age of Freud's time to our contemporary postmodern time emphasizing consumer capitalism. The psychoanalytic patient's unconscious anxieties are not fixed but reflect the broader cultural, political, and socioeconomic context of his/her time, the anxieties and fears that keep him/her up at night. For most people, the unconscious is not a theory of abstract psychological principles; rather, it is what makes us feel frightened, numb, avoidant, creepy, ashamed, secretly aroused, powerful, deeply amused, or fully alive.

Changing Cultural Context of the Unconscious

In the following section, I present a way to think about the changing cultural context and its relationship to the unconscious, the central anxieties and concerns presented by the psychoanalytic patient. Freud's comment that we are not masters in our own house was his way of saying that our actions and conscious understanding are limited by forces outside our control; similarly, we can think of the cultural as a series of forces outside our control and awareness. We might think that unconscious derivatives are only personal and express themselves in an individual's dreams, slips of the tongue, defense mechanisms, and a sense of an alien presence in the self. However, unconscious derivatives also appear in works of art reflecting cultural moments and challenges. I hope to engage the readers of this book in several experiences of the changing cultural framework of the unconscious through an experience of identification. I want to demonstrate these changing perspectives of the unconscious not through an individual's dream but through works of art that we are all familiar with: films. Like dreams, films are visual and contain dramatic plots, polarized themes of good and evil, interesting characters, and powerful visual images, and, like dreams, films provoke intense affect and personal associations. Films reflect the anxieties and fears of a particular time, and the popularity of a film reflects its ability to speak to – evoke – unconscious experiences in the audience.

The films, *Frankenstein*, *Spellbound*, and *World War Z*, reflect the unconscious anxieties, meanings, and structures within three socioeconomic periods that have been critical in the development of psychoanalysis: the early twentieth century, the mid twentieth century, and the late twentieth century. Films, like myths, are communal dreams, expressing our concerns, desires, fears, hopes, dreads, and the 'not me' experiences which fascinate us and which we seek out at the movies. Ezra Klein (2022), a cultural critic, described the way the media, television, social networking, and movies organize and structure our ability to think about the world, providing algorithms for our sense of who we are and what we are afraid of. Like dreams, poetry, and metaphor, films transform and generate conscious and unconscious thought as the stream of visual, verbal, and affective experiences unfolds within diachronic and synchronic time frames.

Frankenstein: *The Unconscious as Other*

Frankenstein; or, the Modern Prometheus, a novel published in 1818 by Mary Shelley (2012), continues to be one of the great works of science fiction and horror in modern times. The power of this novel, the movie, and the many derivative versions of the *Frankenstein* narrative[2] reflect its ability to capture a series of emotional conflicts which have persisted from the early nineteenth century through to the present time, reflecting our fear of our monstrous impulses, of being hated and shunned as an outsider, death, maternal longing, betrayal, and the relationship between science and nature.

I want us to imagine that it is 1931, and we are in a movie theater watching *Frankenstein*. Two scenes horrify and excite us. In the first scene, we are in a dungeon-like space in an old castle – an underground laboratory – surrounded by frightening machines that attempt to capture the energy of a lightning storm. The mad scientist is trying to bring to life a large, humanlike thing which he has assembled from parts of dismembered corpses. In order to reanimate this body, the crazed scientist captures the electrical energy of lightning through the manipulation of an apparatus, which finally makes the body move, act, and live. When he succeeds, he cries out, "It's alive! It's alive!" He soon loses control of the monster, and the citizens of the town become terrified about what this mad scientist has unleashed, reacting with fear and hatred. In the last scene, we see the angry mob setting out with pitchforks and torches to find the monster and kill him.[3]

This film represents the unconscious of the early industrial age. We are afraid of the monster within, afraid of what science, and perhaps psychoanalysis, will release from the depths: an ugly, uncontrollable, murderous monster; an ungainly child who has not learned self-control or the value of delayed gratification. *Franken-stein*, like Freud's early id, reflected a collective terror that arose at the end of the Victorian age, when industrialization, science, urbanization, and industrial capitalism disrupted the agrarian socioeconomic system. With this disruption came the breakdown of prescribed social roles; people no longer knew how they should act or where they belonged. Industrialization created the terror and possibility of change, the loss of traditional communities and social roles, through the separation of wealth from the ownership of land (Brockman, 2010). Neurotic symptoms were marked by inhibitions, repression, fear of desire, struggles with social roles, and, like *Frankenstein*, wanting love, while having uncontrollable, antisocial impulses. This movie and the unconscious cultural pre-scriptions within it resolve these neurotic conflicts by externalizing our monstrous feelings into the primitive Other, finding ways to control or destroy a 'not me' monster who represents the disowned aspects of our unconscious and of ourselves. Asch (1991) traces the evolution of externalized unconscious fears and desires from the witches and devils of agrarian culture to the mad scientist and the evil genius of industrial capitalism, all of which project the unconscious evil into externalized others.[4] During this modernist period, psychoanalysis was in its ascendance and worked to address our fears of the inner monster by offering a rational perspective to counterbalance them, explaining this primitive monster as universal childhood wishes and encouraging a mature, analytical approach involving choice, delay, and sublimation.

Spellbound: *The Unconscious as Confusion of Self and Other*

World War II made us witnesses to the real via the unimaginable horrors of modern war: industrialized murder, state-sponsored hatred, genocide, and the use of science to create nuclear weapons of mass destruction. After the war, it would have been impossible to make a horror film more disturbing than newsreel scenes of concentration camps, the invasion of Normandy, or the nuclear wastelands of Hiroshima and Nagasaki. After WWII, Hollywood turned to noir films in which an anti-hero – a man or woman, in the depths of despair, an alcoholic, a tough guy, a femme fatale –

after failing and losing faith in the world, becomes transformed or redeemed, defeating the corruption within institutions of government, business, and traditional authority. Through the narrative of an individual's personal crisis, noir films presented the underlying cultural crisis of guilt and loss of faith that were the result of WWII. In writing about *Notorious*, a noir film that Hitchcock (1946) and Hecht made after *Spellbound*, Beebe (1990) states that: "it links the unconscious, seemingly personal problem ... to the problem haunting the collective (un)consciousness of its time – guilt for the war." We can think of post-WWII noir films as attempts to express and repair the shared unconscious guilt and broken psyches which came out of WWII. Noir films (Biesen, 2014) fused a subjective, psychological point of view with artistic experimentation influenced by expressionism, surrealism, and documentary realism. In many noir films, this subjective psychological perspective was expressed through elaborate montages, flashbacks, or dreams, revealing the central character's unconscious world and violent obsessions.

Alfred Hitchcock's noir classic, *Spellbound* (Selznick & Hitchcock, 1945), brings together many cultural, sociological, and psychological themes that arose after WWII. Rather than the frightening, mad scientist of the earlier *Frankenstein* narrative who obsesses over the control and alteration of nature, the anti-heroes of noir films embody the individual's internal guilt and identifications, reflecting the political struggles between good and evil, fascism and democracy. Hitchcock presents a positive view of science and psychoanalysis, portraying the psychoanalyst as steadfast, helpful, kind, accepting, and successful.

Spellbound reflects the triumph of psychoanalysis as a cultural institution and a therapeutic practice through which an individual can overcome his/her personal demons and confusion about who he/she actually is. *Spellbound* (Biesen, 2014) opens with a quote from Shakespeare's *Julius Caesar* which emphasizes individual responsibility[5] and the subjective point of view: "The fault ... is not in our stars. But in ourselves," which is immediately followed on-screen by an on-screen introduction describing psychoanalysis as a source of hope and healing.

Hitchcock's view of psychoanalysis emphasized the discovery of hidden truths and interpretation through which rationality and good will would undo the confusion and identifications of self with an evil other,[6] including sadistic political ideologies and guilt over perceived personal failure. Psychoanalysis confirmed the evolving cultural narrative that good had triumphed over evil. This postwar narrative was amplified by rapid socioeconomic changes, including fluidity in social roles, an explosion of scientific knowledge, and a rapidly expanding economic system, all of which contributed to an experience of great optimism. The political monsters had been defeated, and psychoanalysis and the unconscious became part of the public discourse and would show us that we no longer needed to fear our primitive, childlike desires; our unconscious problem was simply that of confusing our identity, not knowing if we are good or evil.

In *Spellbound*, the tormented anti-hero, John Ballantyne (Gregory Peck), cannot remember who he is and believes that he is a murderer in hiding at a sanatorium and pretending to be a psychologist, but he is actually a doctor and WWII veteran suffering from amnesia and guilt. Dr. Brulov, a psychoanalyst, and his assistant, Dr. Constance Petersen (Ingrid Bergman), engage in a Hollywood version of Freudian psychoanalysis, attempting to help their patient discover who he really is. The critical moment in the film occurs within the context of a series of interpretations of a visually powerful, guilt-filled, surrealist nightmare created by Salvador Dali and containing many evocative symbols which leave John Ballantyne convinced and terrified that he is the murderer. Through the analysis of this disturbing dream, Ballantyne reconstructs a repressed memory of a murder he witnessed on a ski slope. However, this is not a simple example of confusion between self and other; Ballantyne's amnesia is linked with his unconscious feelings of guilt in relation to his brother's death when they were children. The analyst's interpretations lift the curtain of amnesia that had separated Ballantyne from his real identity as a good person and not a murderer; he is no longer confused and lost. This noir movie, like many others, validated the postwar optimism and belief that humans are essentially good and not evil, which helped to resolve the postwar guilt, creating a new, optimistic, heroic narrative along with contemporary definitions of the unconscious and psychoanalysis. Insight now involved the discovery that we are not the evil murderer, the child/monster that we believed we were; we were only confusing our self with an evil Other.

World War Z: The Unconscious as Not Feeling Alive, a Loss of Individuality and Subjectivity

The movies of our time, like the news media, are filled with apocalyptic visions, fear rather than optimism and victory over the evil Other. We are victims under constant attack, and the fundamental question is whether humankind will survive this perpetual onslaught. Reviewers (Denby, 2013) of *Night of the Living Dead* (Hardman, Streiner, and Romero, 1968), an early zombie film, note that it represented an important shift from traditional horror movies in which the victims are attacked because they did something wrong (punishment); in these zombie films, death and destruction are random: the attack is on being human, on being alive. Nothing holds the key to salvation – not family, not love, not law. Zombie films (D'Costa, 2011) present a vision of contemporary unconscious anxieties, our struggle to create meaning, to have hope, and the psychological question of whether we are dead or alive.

World War Z (2013) begins with a young family trying to finish breakfast so that the parents can take their two children to school and get on with their busy day. As is typical for many families, the morning news is streaming in the background while they eat. Reports of terrifying events, death, and destruction in all corners of the world are a background flood of information as they hurriedly eat breakfast. The family leaves for school and work, becoming stuck in what appears to be an ordinary morning traffic jam, which suddenly turns into a terrifying attack: their first exposure to the plague of zombies. The zombies careen through the stuck traffic, banging their heads on car windows, which crack open like clam shells, allowing the zombies to eat the flesh of the commuters. After they are bitten, people quickly turn into zombies as they become infected by the virus. Brad Pitt, the hero of the film, is terrified and desperately attempts to save his family.

Soon he is petitioned by a former colleague, a United Nations official, who promises him that his family will be kept safe if he agrees to go on a mission to find the first case of this plague so that a cure can be found. Most of the world has already fallen to the plague of zombies, and the remaining, uninfected population is living safely in isolation on an aircraft carrier. This film articulates a new anxiety, and through the psychological subtext of the movie we see that Brad Pitt's terror is not only of the zombies, but that his children will lose their subjective identities and become part of an impersonal mob, the walking dead, zombies with insatiable appetites. This film suggests that our greatest fear is not of our externalized unconscious wishes, or a confusion between ourselves and evildoers, but that we will become creatures without an inner life, without personal meaning, incapable of experiencing pleasure, compulsively consuming without satisfaction.[7]

Zombie films reflect the anxieties inherent in the contemporary culture of consumer capitalism, which depends on constant consumption, in contrast to traditional industrial capitalism, which emphasized the delay of gratification and the accumulation and production of wealth. This change from industrial capitalism to consumer capitalism can be seen as an intentional government strategy in countries such as China, where millions of rural people were moved from their homes and villages into newly built urban centers where their economic function is no longer to create 'wealth' but to embody and support consumerism. This cultural shift – the demand to consume, to enjoy – is more starkly presented in totalitarian countries where it is an explicit policy, rather than in democracies, where the forces of economic control and planning remain opaque, although equally effective.

Lacan conceptualizes (Böhm & Batta, 2010) socioeconomic structures as systems of enjoyment where pleasure develops differently in the three registers of experience: the imaginary, the symbolic, and the real. Consumer capitalism (Stein, 2011) is understood primarily within the imaginary register, the mirror stage, in which the image, the illusion of being perfect, of being the thing that makes the Mother complete – the winner, the survivor, the hero – is experienced anew with each object purchased. We become disappointed and need our next new thing, our next fix, as we turn to our next hoped-for promise of happiness. Cycles of hoped-for pleasure and disappointment are continuous and represent moment-to-moment attempts to reconstitute the self and hold the self together within the mirror stage, enacted within the socioeconomic structure of consumer capitalism. Purchasing a new suit or a new dress results in a moment of pleasure as we see ourself reflected in both real and imaginary mirrors; however, this pleasure is momentary before the disappointment and emptiness return, as they do in all addictions, where pleasure is a promise that will be ours at some future moment but not now. We become numb, like the walking dead, as we learn through repeating experiences, like an addict or a zombie, that there is nothing but hunger without satisfaction. The cultural imperative is to enjoy, tying individuals into continuous cycles of consumption. We become zombies who consume without satisfaction, part of a mindless, de-subjectified mob, consuming as a way to escape from the emptiness, deadness, lack of meaning, impotence, and cynicism about culture, government, and other institutions. Zombie movies, such as *World War Z*, reflect profound cultural changes (Lewis, 2011) in the socioeconomic system that have affected the structure of the unconscious and our sense of who we are, our capacity to generate personal meaning, and the lack of hope that underlies contemporary fears and anxieties, signifying a loss of subjectivity, becoming 'nothing,' much like the walking dead wandering through an apocalyptic world, consuming without satisfaction, living from moment to moment, and constantly questioning whether we are alive or dead, which reflects a profound sense of emptiness and a lack of the unconscious capacity to dream and create intimacy.

Concluding Comments

I hope that this book will enhance clinicians' ability to understand the historical dimensions of their work with patients and their understanding of the psychological concept of the unconscious. As a clinician and professor, I find myself fascinated by all of these theories and believe that I work mostly from a broad relational approach which is deeply immersed in Kleinian and developmental theories, but, as must be obvious, I really love theory and hope that you will too!

Notes

1 Typically, one would say conscious and unconscious thought; however, I prefer the concept of experience, to include non-linguistic products of both conscious and unconscious processes.
2 A contemporary version of the *Frankenstein* narrative is presented as an analysis of the film *The Skin I Live In* (Lema, 2012), where the mad scientist, now a mad plastic surgeon, attempts to create a replacement for the traumatic losses of his wife and daughter. This essay presents three intersecting explanations for our time: a perverse Oedipal drama, a breakdown of the capacity for symbolization, and an emphasis on the body as a commodity, emphasizing the imaginary register over the symbolic.
3 In its last scene, *King Kong* (Cooper, Schoedsack, & Selznick, 1933) is another film that follows the *Frankenstein* narrative, where the frightened crowd also destroys the beast, who represents unconscious desire and nature (Whale, 1931).
4 *The Manchurian Candidate* (Axelrod & Frankenheimer, 1962) also uses a *Frankenstein* narrative with an important change in the source of danger, from the mad scientist and evil genius of industrial capitalism to the racial or political other of the post-WWII period.
5 This quote within the context of this iconic noir film brings to mind Shafer's (1976) arguments in *A New Language for Psychoanalysis*.
6 The literature on identification with the aggressor (Freud, 1936) and Ferenczi's (1988) paper, "A Confusion of Tongues between the Adult and Child," develop this psychoanalytic emphasis on identification and the confusion in identifications between the good self and the evil other.
7 I think that the Rolling Stones (Jagger & Richards, 1965) song "(I Can't Get No) Satisfaction" is a similar commentary on contemporary culture.

Chapter 1

The Evolution of Freud's Theories of the Unconscious

Introduction

Freud's personal and intellectual development was steeped in the scientific method of modernism and the simultaneous growth of industrialization. Both cultural trends emphasized the subordination of nature and the substitution of rational thought for irrational beliefs. As a student of anatomy and neurology, Freud struggled with differences between the functioning of the brain, a biological entity, and the mind, a psychological organization. In his work with people diagnosed as hysterics, it became clear that their symptoms did not follow known neurological pathways but rather seemed to function as non-verbal forms of memory and meaning. Many of Freud's struggles involved the tension between these two epistemological systems, biology and psychology, and his inability to completely align himself with one or the other.

Freud's writing reflects different intentions: sharing his experience of discovery, systematizing these discoveries into complex, multidimensional theories describing the functioning of the mind, suggestions for clinical practice, and finally a political or perhaps evangelical project in which he presented the universal importance of his discoveries: the unconscious and the talking cure. The political or evangelical dimension of Freud's work underlines the unfortunate tradition of 'excommunicating' colleagues seen as heretics, beginning with many of his early followers and continuing into present-day arguments about the pursuit of legitimacy in psychoanalysis. However, many contemporary psychoanalysts do

DOI: 10.4324/9781003058274-2

not have Freud's ironic temperament which leavened his missionary zeal, as when he said, on entering New York Harbor, "I am bringing the plague to America."

Freud's concept of the unconscious evolved alongside his work with patients, moving from simple concepts of the unconscious as reflecting singular moments of emotional dysregulation which resulted in mysterious symptoms to complex organizations of interdependent mental structures which struggled to maintain their integrity, a form of homeostasis, maintaining patients' symptoms, unhappiness, and resistance to change. I want to emphasize how each development in the concept of the unconscious grew out of a change in Freud's work with patients, which led to further developments in conceptualizing the structure of the mind. This was a beneficial cycle which began with Freud's practice and resulted in the development of theory which then led to the further development within the psychoanalytic method. In the following sections, I want to describe the evolution of the structural dimensions of the unconscious and highlight the clinical work which led to these developments. Each of the following discoveries were additive, expanding the previous conceptualizations, and were not attempts to replace earlier versions of the concept of the unconscious with later versions. Freud was 'discovering' the expanding universe of our inner worlds, and his ability to understand and create more complex systems was quite exciting and exceptional.

Freud (1901) never tired of illustrating the presence of unconscious organizations of experience, attempting to normalize these experiences with examples from everyday life and continuing towards an almost postmodern understanding of the importance of creating narratives (Freud, 1935). To put it simply, Freud was trying to make us aware of aspects of mind which we wished not to know. He (Freud, 1917) wanted to highlight the idea that, "The ego is not master in its own house" but is often pressed to act by forces outside awareness, which we think of as the unconscious.

From phenomenological and experiential perspectives, the unconscious is the area of the unknown, of surprise, of mystery, of uncertainty, of incomprehensible action often experienced as the emergence of an alien presence, in word, feeling, or action. I would like to illustrate the emergence of an unconscious experience revealing a truth that a patient wished not to know, which was revealed by an embarrassing slip of the tongue. An analysand who was insisting that he takes our work seriously used the word levity instead of gravity to describe how seriously he took our work. Over the next several minutes, he repeated the word levity in different versions of the same statement. Finally, he said, "did I say levity?" which I affirmed, and we both began to laugh. Becoming aware of his verbal slip, as if it was an alien object that flew out of his mouth, helped him see his complicated feelings about analysis, as he enacted a continuing resistance to seeing his unconscious participation in this and other parts of his life.

Clinical Origins of Psychic Structure and the Unconscious

In the late nineteenth century, many physicians were using hypnosis to treat hysteria, which, as Szasz (2010) commented about Freud, was a monumental humanistic and scientific step beyond seeing hysterical patients (usually women) as morally flawed or congenitally weak. Freud began working with hysterical patients using hypnosis, attempting to facilitate their remembering forgotten experiences which would result in catharsis and instantly eliminate their symptoms (Breuer and Freud,1893/1957). Freud adopted the "pressure technique," a form of hypnotic suggestion, in which he would place his hand on a patient's head and say that, when he released his hand, the patient would remember the moment or experience in which his/her hysterical symptom arose.[1] However, he quickly moved away from hypnosis, stating that it was unreliable and, perhaps more importantly, he responded to his patients' wishes to not be forced to remember on demand. I believe that this shift in technique from hypnosis and direct suggestion to an early collaborative relationship was a revolutionary moment in history and the beginning of psychoanalysis. Freud reoriented his therapeutic stance from being an authority, being the doctor in charge of the treatment, towards a more collaborative process in which he asked patients to talk about what came to their minds and their associations to particular events in the past.

This shift in clinical technique led to patients being treated with greater respect and autonomy and the development of the free association method and psychoanalysis.

The dualistic model of the mind, implicit in hypnosis, involved the presence and absence of memories and set the stage for Freud's development of the topographic model of the mind. The topographic model describes conscious and unconscious areas of experience within a hierarchical system in which the forgotten, unconscious experiences lay beneath conscious awareness. The analyst's job was to bring the 'forgotten' memories, affects, and meanings into conscious awareness, allowing these unconscious experiences to become integrated into the fabric of the individual's life. According to Abend (2007), this early theory evolved into a far more sophisticated derivative during the first two decades of the twentieth century, with the topographic model of the mind forming the basis for Freud's ideas about mental structure and functioning. Within the topographic model, the mind was conceptualized as a hierarchical system in which memories existed in an unconscious form that needed to be brought into a higher level of conscious thought where they could be addressed in a rational, secondary process manner. The idea of depth and the goal of making the unconscious conscious reflect the influence of the topographic model.

Freud initially conceptualized the unconscious as an organization of memories (thing presentations) of unacceptable wishes and infantile impulses which were closed off from conscious awareness (words) as a result of traumatic experiences in which the individual was overwhelmed by affect and unable to integrate their experience. The theory of the traumatic etiology of hysteria became more specifically organized around sexual trauma. During this early period of the development of the topographic model, the etiology of hysteria moved from general trauma to sexually based trauma and then to the seduction theory (Blass & Simon, 1994). Blass and Simon (1994) describe Freud's development of the seduction theory as involving the following course: an earlier, prepubescent event that stimulated the child's genitals is not represented until it becomes reactivated when a postpubertal sexual event or seduction[2] occurs which revives the memory of the earlier seduction – sexual event – which must be defended against and not allowed into consciousness, resulting in the neurosis.

Freud modified the seduction theory, which initially described any sexual event, to always be the result of an incestuous relationship with the father. Blass and Simon (1994) present Freud's argument that, without the presumption of an infantile "pre-sexual sexual event" (1896a), it would be impossible to understand the neurosis. For, as Freud explains, "no hysterical symptom can arise from a real experience alone" (1896b, p. 197). However, Freud (Blass & Simon, 1994) began to doubt his formulation of paternal seduction, an extension of the earlier trauma theory, questioning the reality of his patients' memories and considering the possibility that the therapist's suggestion played a part in eliciting patients' memories. Freud began to suspect that some of his patients' 'memories' of paternal seduction might have been based on fantasies rather than on actual events.

This change in his understanding of the etiology of hysteria represented a growing awareness of the place of fantasy (Abend, 2008) in unconscious representations. Freud (1925) noted the similarity between his patients' memories of paternal seduction and the stories of sexual abuse by the devil allegedly confessed to by 'witches' during the Middle Ages. Freud (1925) courageously notes that his patients' reports of their fathers' acts were in accord with his own seductive fantasies directed towards his parents, daughter, and patients. These and other factors caused Freud to suggest that Oedipal fantasies were a universal aspect of the unconscious which generated the fantasies, which became a substitute for the trauma theory and the seduction theory. Freud's adoption of the Oedipal narrative is interesting in that it seems to support his political intention to make his observations universal while also altering the narrative of the Greek tragedy to conform with his one-person perspective, reflecting the child's fantasy and leaving out the father's fears, fantasies, and murderous wishes. Alternatively, the Oedipal trilogy can be seen as a family drama in which the father/parent is frightened by the child's budding sexuality and autonomy[3] or as a representation of a complex cultural and gender-based Oedipal narrative[4] describing a struggle between the authority of the state and that of the family.

Freud's monumental discovery in the course of his early analyses and self-analysis was the recognition that unconscious fantasy can be experienced as real and can determine who we are and
organize our experience, behavior, desires, and choices in the real
world. This shift from the theory of paternal seduction, an outgrowth of the early trauma theory, to the central importance of
fantasy and Oedipal desires created a concept of the unconscious
that was not simply reactive to external events but had its own
internal system of motivation (energy) which was able to organize
a person's identity, neurosis, and conflict. This reflected a shift
from a reactive to a proactive concept of the unconscious in
which desire and the individual's fantasies become important
motivational elements standing alongside biological drives.
Freud continued to struggle with the comparative importance of
external and internal reality as he continued to expand his theory
into a tripartite model of conscious, unconscious, and preconscious
structures.

Resistance, Repression, and Working Through

Freud's belief that patients wanted to get well and would welcome
his interpretations which would lead to relief from their symptoms
was sadly tested; he discovered that the mind was far less rational
and more complex than a simple energy discharge system which
the positivist perspective that dominated nineteenth-century science predicted. Patients resisted understanding and change; they
worked hard to hold on to their neurotic forms of unhappiness.
Freud's case of Dora (1905), which has drawn much criticism,
stands at the crossroads of Freud's final revision of his motivational and structural theories, including the movement away from
the seduction theory and the topographic model to the structural
model in which he developed the clinical concepts of resistance
and its metapsychological counterpart, repression. This model
conceptualized the unconscious as an active system having its own
organization and dynamics, functioning in a proactive manner,
rather than simply reacting to external events. In his work with
Dora, Freud discovered that analysis could be an adversarial
experience, and that he, the analyst, was subject to unconscious

field forces that resulted in his reenacting the relationships that the patient was describing within the newly emerging experience of transference. The concept of transference (Abend, 2009) and the awareness that simply remembering is not enough but that psychoanalytic therapy necessitates a reliving of the dynamic relational structures of the past in the present therapeutic relationship formed the critical step in further developments of psychoanalytic treatment.

Ahbel-Rappe (2009, p. 597) carefully deconstructs Freud's Dora paper, describing how it represented an important but difficult change in Freud's view of mental structure, now emphasizing fantasy and repression in contrast to the seduction theory.

> [D]espite Freud's questioning of the seduction theory in his letters to Fliess, Freud did not actually abandon the seduction theory altogether; rather, seduction took its etiological place in the context of Freud's expanded etiological outlook. It was now fantasy and repression instead of trauma and seduction after 1897.

Although the Dora paper is written with a contemptuous attitude towards Dora, reenacting the abusive behavior and attitudes of Dora's father and Herr K., Freud is able to use these experiences to expand his theory, now emphasizing that Dora had the status of an intentional agent, a subject who had her own motivation and was not simply reactive. He expanded the libido theory to be an endogenous source of energy reflected in early sexual experiences of masturbation; fantasies and desires of the individual as a subject and not simply an object reacting to sexual abuse. In this case history, we can see Freud beginning to come to terms with questions of transference and how, if he had been willing to provide a more compassionate attitude, this might have changed the course of the analysis. Unfortunately, this recognition came after he, like Herr K., felt rejected by Dora and was unable to recognize his own reaction to being rejected by this deeply hurt adolescent girl.

Freud's conflicts about Dora as a sexualized adolescent or about giving up the seduction theory were clearly resolved by the time he wrote the "Rat Man" case history (Freud, 1909). Here, we see a compassionate analyst who allowed and entered into a full transference experience in which he became both the cruel and loving father that he and the patient co-created within the analysis.

This shift from an authority who emphasizes the truth of his interpretations, harking back to the pressure technique and topographic model, to collaborator who is subject to the 'rules of analysis' is wonderfully illustrated in the Rat Man case (Freud, 1909), when the patient asks Freud to be allowed to not describe an embarrassing incident, and Freud states:

> Here the patient broke off, got up from the sofa, and begged me to spare him the recital of the details. I assured him that I myself had no taste whatever for cruelty, and certainly had no desire to torment him, but that naturally I could not grant him something which was beyond my power.[5] He might just as well ask me to give him the moon. The overcoming of resistances was a law of the treatment, and on no consideration could it be dispensed with.
>
> (p. 165)

Freud's statement can be seen as referring to both the analytic situation, where overcoming resistance is the fundamental activity, and the tripartite mental structure where repression and censorship organize mental activity, neurotic symptoms, and the narrative of one's history. The analyst is not simply focused on the patient remembering forgotten events, memories, but is now interested in a whole system of unconscious thought and becomes a facilitator or guide in the discovery of unconscious dynamics. The analysis is no longer simply focused on the recovery of memories, but on understanding the metonymy of the patient's symptoms and personality structure – in this case, the repetitive schemas of the patient's family, personality, transference, and analysis.

Throughout his work, Freud struggled with understanding unconscious memories, believing that their recovery was the key to analytic work. His positivist view of the mind led him to believe that memories existed as units in the unconscious, perhaps like lost photographs, which could be found and brought into consciousness. In an interesting paper (Freud, 1915a), he argues that the mental representation of a memory exists separated into two parts, a verbal part and an action or affective part, which had become separated through the mechanism of repression. The act of remembering involved the reintegration of these two parts which involved both a cathartic process and a moment of insight, an 'ah ha moment' in which the patient suddenly realized the meaning of a symptom or unconscious causal sequence. Unfortunately, Freud found that his patients often did not remember these earlier events, or, when they did, they minimized the importance of these memories. In one of his last papers, Freud (1937) approached what we may think of as a postmodern perspective on memories, differentiating interpretation as involving a single event or memory and construction as a somewhat creative narrative of what might have happened in the patient's past which led to the current situation. This idea of a narrative construction, like a personal myth, involves the patient experiencing a high degree of belief and finding the construction to be more than plausible. In this paper, Freud (1937) uses the archaeological metaphor, comparing the unconscious and the analyst's activity to an archaeologist constructing a model of a historical city from the shards of pottery and broken columns found at a dig.

Freud's view of the mind as an archaeological site emphasized the contents of past events, memories, which through complex processes of repression were placed outside conscious thought into the unconscious system (UCS). Freud (1917) developed an alternative view of the mental structure based on dreams and their function in the mind. He understood dreams as the map for the unconscious involving dual processes of representation, primary and secondary process thought – how the mind created meaning differently in the UCS and the pre-conscious system (PCS). In today's language, we may think of processes of representation as the rules or algorithms through which experiences, both conscious and unconscious, are transformed into thoughts and meaningful experiences. Freud's most complete discussions of unconscious processes of thought were presented in *The Interpretation of Dreams* (Freud, 1900) and his subsequent writings on dreams, humor, and the psychopathology of everyday life. Freud described this process of dream formation from a metapsychological perspective in which he restates his view of the dynamics of the separation of the thing (action or affect) and word aspects of an experience:

> We have already in *The Interpretation of Dreams* [Standard Ed., 5, 542 ff.] described the way in which the regression of the preconscious day's residues takes place in dream-formation. In this process thoughts are transformed into images, mainly of a visual sort; that is to say, word-presentations are taken back to the thing-presentations which correspond to them, as if, in general, the process were dominated by considerations of representability [Standard Ed., 5, 548]. When regression has been completed, a number of cathexes are left over in the UCS – cathexes of memories of things. The primary psychical process is brought to bear on these memories, till, by condensation of them and displacement between their respective cathexes, it has shaped the manifest dream-content. Only where the word-presentations occurring in the day's residues are recent and current residues of perceptions, and not the expression of thoughts, are they themselves treated like thing-presentations, and subjected to the influence of condensation and displacement.

The clinical process of dream interpretation involved the patient associating to each element of the dream and the analyst facilitating the movement from the manifest dream to the dream thoughts. This was largely a process of translation from an element of the dream to articulating the unconscious meaning of the dream through a recognition of the underlying wishes which were distorted by primary process mentation. The goal was to bring the primary process representations into a more rational understanding of the unconscious wish. In order to understand this process of dream interpretation, it is important to understand the primary process of unconscious representation.

Freud (1915b) described the primary processes – the form of representation that occurs in unconscious thought – as having the following characteristics:

- Lacking mutual contradiction; opposites could exist side by side.
- No negation, no doubt, only different levels of intensity.
- Condensation and displacement of one idea for another, which is a hallmark of primary process.
- When primary process is able to directly affect the secondary process of CNS (the conscious system) or PCS, "it appears comic and excites laughter" (p. 186).
- Timelessness, not ordered by time and have no reference to time.
- Has little regard for reality and operates on the demands of the pleasure principle.
- Replacement of external reality by psychic reality.
- UCS experience is knowable through symptoms, dreams, and somatic reactions.

Without changing his view on how experiences are represented in the unconscious, Freud (1920) altered his view on the motivation of dreams, recognizing that dreams do not always represent wish fulfillment. Freud (1920) confronted more complex unconscious experiences represented in both dreams and behavior, some of which came out of World War I, including post-traumatic dreams which repeated experiences of horror and required Freud to acknowledge that these dreams could not represent a wish fulfillment but some other process. He (Freud, 1920) suggested that both traumatic and repetitive dreams represented a different unconscious process, something like a failure in symbolization, and that these repetitive experiences needed to be worked through, repeating the traumatic experience within a different affective context. He illustrates this process of working through by describing his observation of his grandson's creating the Fort Da game, in which, through joyful repetition of making a toy go away and come back, he mastered the trauma of his mother's leaving and returning.

Dimensions of the Unconscious

In concluding this chapter I want to schematically identify six dimensions or characteristics that Freud (1915b) conceptualized in his development of the structural model of the mind which he thought of as consisting of the three systems, CNS, PCS, and UCS, later defined as the ego, superego, and id. These structures were thought of as organized in a hierarchy in which reality-focused, conscious, rational thought was privileged over unconscious, irrational, or emotional thought. I present these six dimensions of Freud's view of psychic structure to highlight the complexity of his thinking and to provide a model to think about subsequent views of mental structure and the unconscious which will be presented in the following chapters.

1   The topographic model separated conscious from unconscious experience, instantiating a hierarchical relationship between conscious and unconscious thought. Memories became unconscious as the result of unacceptable, intense emotional experiences and could be reintegrated into conscious experience through suggestion or interpretation. This was a reactive view of the unconscious in which the main motivational factor was severe emotional discomfort or, conceptually, the discharge of affect/ energy and the maintenance of homeostasis. The unremembered affective, unacceptable event operated like an infection, and the analyst's interpretation was seen as draining the infection through a process of emotional release or catharsis.

2   The structural model described the complex relationships between the conscious system (CNS), the unconscious system (UCS), and the pre-conscious system (PCS), recognizing internal processes or forces such as "censorship" and "repression" which determined the fate of memory, thought, and action. Rather than being reactive, this was becoming a proactive system involving a form of agency, or choice, which incorporated independent motivational systems including the realization that fantasy and desire created conflicts among the structural systems, including reality, represented by the superego. Simple cathartic release and remembering became a complex process of working through the many instances of a pathological schema.

3   Developmental and motivational models described stages of libidinal development, beginning with traumatic narratives of sexual abuse during the early topographic model which

extended into the seduction model, in which early sexual abuse by the father became central, and, as Freud became aware of the importance of fantasy, he hypothesized a universal Oedipal narrative as the apex of his libidinal model of motivation. These developmental and motivational models involved a clash between the individual's desire (the pleasure principle) and the demands of society (the reality principle).

4   An evolving understanding of memory focused on a shift from a simple verbal process to behavioral actions as a representation of a repressed desire and as a form of remembering and, finally, into a process of constructing plausible histories as opposed to discovering actual memories of events. It was necessary to construct reasonable narratives instead of veridical memories and consider the influence of the past on present experience (transference) and that of the present on past experience (countertransference) in constructing memories and personal narratives.

5   Models of representation in conscious and unconscious mentation and experience included dreams, humor, slips of the tongue, and an expansion of the concepts of primary and secondary process thinking. Discussions of representation in conscious and unconscious mentation (cognition) expanded the structural model beyond the emphasis on energy dynamics towards an emphasis on meaning and how it is created in the different structures of the mind.

Notes

1   I think of the similarity between this technique and the development of free association.
2   The word seduction is used to represent any experience which may arouse sexual feeling, from "a brush of the knee to consummated incest."
3   See Kohut's (1984) discussion in *How Does Analysis Cure?*
4   See Fromm's (1951) discussion in *The Forgotten Language.*
5   I always find this comment to be very interesting. I believe that Freud is speaking in an ironic voice, but he is also establishing a form of neutrality in which he emphasizes curiosity and understanding over influence and cure.

Chapter 2

The Unconscious in Interpersonal and Relational Psychoanalysis

Introduction

This chapter describes the unconscious in interpersonal and relational psychoanalysis. The question of whether these are separate theories or relational psychoanalysis is an evolution of interpersonal psychoanalysis is more of a political question than a theoretical one. I will explore the many overlapping concepts and clinical approaches shared by both theories while recognizing important differences between these approaches. A more important issue for these theories is the difficulty in using psychoanalytic structural concepts, such as the unconscious, because interpersonal and relational theories emphasize pragmatic and phenomenological approaches, eschewing the use of abstract systems of theoretical propositions. Both interpersonal and relational theories privilege experience-near approaches to psychoanalytic practice and theory, emphasizing the uniqueness of each analytic pair over universal, metapsychological systems of thought. However, I believe that it is not possible to work as a therapist or analyst without having a set of theoretical propositions which organize clinical work, whether explicit or implicit, and it is important to understand the underlying theoretical structures which organize each theory and therapeutic approach. I will try to articulate the theoretical propositions which organize the clinical work of interpersonal and relational analysts, particularly how they understand unconscious processes in their work with patients.

DOI: 10.4324/9781003058274-3

The Evolution of Interpersonal Psychoanalysis

Interpersonal psychoanalysis was developed by Harry Stack Sullivan, with important contributions by Clara Thompson and Erich Fromm. These authors focused on the importance of clinical work and how patients' difficulties in living (Sullivan, 1970), their character structure, or diagnosis influenced the clinical process with different categories of patients. Sullivan (Havens, 1976), having been strongly influenced by American culture and philosophy,[1] was primarily interested in facilitating therapeutic change, taking a pragmatic approach to both clinical work and theory. Havens (1976) illustrates an important and perhaps iconic difference between the practice of classical and interpersonal psychoanalysis, describing how Sullivan literally positioned himself alongside his patient, rather than behind the couch, in order to see the world from his patient's perspective while attempting to expand the experiential and perceptual world of that patient. For Sullivan and other interpersonal theorists, it was the necessity to adapt to the implicit and explicit demands in the interpersonal world, rather than the necessity to control inner drives and infantile impulses, that was the origin of psychopathology and the key to understanding patients' motivational systems. Sullivan shared this perspective, focusing on the patient's actual experience in the external world, with other post-Freudian theorists (Monroe, 1955) who rejected Freud's biological and mechanical perspectives, including drive theory and metapsychology, focusing instead on problems in living which were a result of adaptation to the fear and anxiety present in the environment that distorted the individual's development. Sullivan preferred the term 'problems in living,' which reflected the distortions of one's being, of one's self-structure, and were the result of one's experience of the other's, the parent's or caretaker's, anxiety. For Sullivan and other interpersonal theorists, anxiety shaped the child's self-structure, a system of operations which were organized to avoid the occurrence of anxiety, finding security through shrinking or narrowing the self and experience. The self-system[2] was a series of operations that led to the possibility of safety and security rather than being overwhelmed by anxiety in the interpersonal world. Psychopathology was defined as a narrowing of the self-structure and the interpersonal field, limiting possible activities and thoughts that the individual could participate in or allow into awareness, redefining the concept of the unconscious as an organization of unattended experiences and unthought ideas and experiences. Sullivan saw the self-system's function as avoiding anxiety in both action and thought. Sullivan (1953, p. 56), like Freud, was a master in the use of metaphor and presented his understanding of the self-system through describing the tragedy that most people experience in their lives as: "I believe that for a great majority of our people, preadolesence is the nearest that they come to untroubled human life – that from then on, the stresses of life distort them to inferior caricatures of what they might have been."

It is interesting to compare Sullivan's early ideas about the self-system with Freud's topographic model. Both theories call attention to the division of consciousness, of awareness, the separation of what can be known from what is not known. However, for Sullivan, that which is not known, the unconscious, is not stored in a virtual file cabinet, buried in an archaeological site, or actively excluded from consciousness through repression, but it is never learned, is never articulated in language, and continues to be avoided or acted on without conscious awareness. Consciousness, for Sullivan, functions to both know things and to avoid knowing things; it is a limiting function of attentional processes which he described as selective (in)attention. Unlike Freud, but like many other neo-Freudian theorists (Monroe, 1955), Sullivan saw anxiety as a product of implicit and explicit interpersonal experience – criticisms, fears, and rebukes which mostly remain unknown to the person because of processes of selective inattention; a product of avoiding knowing and not wanting to know what is occurring in the environment but has shaped the self-system, the personality. Sullivan used the concept of "not me" as a way of recognizing the individual's disowned actions, feelings, and thoughts. The comedian Flip Wilson captured the joyful surprise of the disowned 'not me' experience: when being confronted by the dissociated and unattended aspects of his action, he stated: "The Devil Made Me Do It."

Sullivan developed the technique of the detailed inquiry through which he would try to fill in those parts of experience which had been excluded from awareness by anxiety. Some inter-personal practitioners present this technique as confrontational, and some stay closer to Sullivan, who was a master at using non-verbal aspects of speech, including exaggeration, hyperbole, humor, and what developmental psychologists refer to as marked speech (Fonagy & Target, 2007). For Sullivan, the detailed inquiry was part of a collaborative approach in which he would first try to help his patient feel less anxious and sensitized to criticism, often poking implicit and explicit fun at himself. Sullivan (1970, p. 8) described patients' experience of his therapeutic approach in the following way:

> I do not believe that I have had an interview with anybody in twenty-five years in which the person to whom I was talking was not annoyed during the early part of the interview by my asking stupid questions.

Sullivan's use of "stupid questions" was not simply an aspect of the technique of the detailed inquiry (Appelbaum, 2010; Aron, 1989; Bromberg, 1993; Hirsch, 1992) but reflected his belief that, when patients come to therapy, they suffer from anxiety about being seen as inadequate and feel potentially humiliated by asking for help. Sullivan (1970) wanted to emphasize the common experience of shared humanity (Crowley, 1978), of not seeing himself (the analyst) as superior, and his (Sullivan, 2013, p. 18) belief that: "We are all much more simply human than otherwise, be we happy and successful, contented and detached, miserable and mentally disordered, or whatever," expressing a sense of shared humanity which he conceptualized as consensual valida-tion (Bromberg, 1980) and collaboration in the psychoanalytic relationship.

Sullivan thought of consensual validation initially as a devel-opmental process of moving from the restricted emotional context of the family, a world of particular emotional experience, to the discovery that other families have their own ways of doing things. Within this expanding context of experience, the child becomes able to share his inner experiences and anxieties with a friend, a chum. Because of this "chum-ship experience" and experiences of consensual validation, the child is able to move from a self- and family-centered, fearful view of the world (parataxic thinking) to a more socially normative view of the world (syntactic thinking), reducing the anxieties developed in the world of the family. Oftentimes, people who suffer from severe psychopathology have not had a chumship experience and continue to see the external world as a narrow and frightening place.

Sullivan did not have an explicit concept of the unconscious, but rather focused on the limitations that the self-system placed on the patient's awareness and being. Levenson (1981, 2003), one of the most prolific and important second-generation interpersonal theorists, has frequently elaborated the critical importance of expanding the patient's self-awareness through the use of the detailed inquiry. He (Levenson, 2003) has compared the detailed inquiry to postmodern deconstruction, expanding and generating new meaning, and has emphasized that the process of the detailed inquiry is a largely visual process[3] emphasizing that, as analysts, we are trying to visualize what the patient is describing in language. The detailed inquiry moves from more abstract verbal productions to more specific and concrete visual images, which, along with Levenson, we (Newirth, 2018; Schore, 2011) may think of as reflecting right-brain functions, non-verbal patterns, schemas, or dreamlike images. Levenson (1988) believes that the task of analysis is not to make sense of the patient's narrative[4] but to resist this process of making sense, leaving the situation open for an evolving creative understanding. He states:

> It is my contention that the impulse of the analytic process emerges from just this forcing of data; i.e., the deconstruction of the patient's prepared text, the clinical material, rather than the analyst's explanation of the plethora of data which emerges. I suspect that this is the analytic vis a tergo, the driving force, regardless of the metapsychological imagery used. In short, one is not simply collating a lot of information which can then, leisurely, be composed by analyst and patient into a "good story" – one which fulfills their requirement for an aesthetic, plausible and inclusive version of events ... The very act of fragmenting the patient's fictionalized version of his/her

life causes anxiety and promotes the transferential carryover. Why this should be so is not so clear to me. The traditional view is that by speaking of that which is supposed to be left unspoken (inattended, repressed), one is pushing against the defenses, forcing an enrichment of the defensive surface story, and provoking the transfer of both the content and the defenses into the analyst–patient relationship. But, I suspect, that what is "repressed" is not so straightforward or linear, and that defenses are not so clear about what they are defending against. It may not be all that reasonable. The very breakdown of narrative order, the temporary chaos which is provoked, may, in itself, be vital to a creative process, a reorganization of experience into far more complex and flexible patterns.

(p. 5)

The interpersonal psychoanalytic approach does not simply focus on the deconstruction and expansion of the patient's narrative but refocuses the process on the analytic interaction, understanding that the analyst's reactions to the patient can reasonably be understood as an induced countertransference reaction. Many of the theorists involved in the development of interpersonal psychoanalysis focused on the immediacy of the transference–countertransference relationship, incorporating the language and concepts of object relations theorists (Racker, 1982; Searles, 1979) and articulating their own versions of the experience between patient and therapist. Levenson and other interpersonal theorists described three isomorphic transformations in the analytic narratives: the story of the patient's childhood, the story of their current relationships, and the story of the analytic relationship. Often, as the treatment proceeds, the analytic relationship takes center stage, and the stories of childhood and current relationships recede towards the periphery.

I would like to illustrate the process of this movement from the patient's history to its being enacted in the analytic relationship with an example presented by Bromberg (1996), who can be identified as both an interpersonal and a relational psychoanalyst. To use a metaphor which he (Bromberg, 1996) likes, his work

stands in both spaces, both theoretical realms, and would seemingly support the view of relational psychoanalysis as an evolution of interpersonal psychoanalysis. In the following example,
Bromberg, in keeping with the interpersonal perspective, is essentially understanding his patient as having been molded by his
mother's powerful image, and, in the therapeutic enactment,
Bromberg takes on the parental role of knowing how his patient
should be. In addition, as the enactment develops, the patient
takes on the role of shaming the other, inverting his own experience by shaming Bromberg, as he has often felt shamed. The
example illustrates the concept of the unconscious not as series of
memories but as patterns of behavior which occur outside awareness and are brought into consciousness in the analytic dialogue,
not through interpretation but as a performative enactment in
which both analyst and patient cannot help but see and react to
the unspoken reality that is organizing this complex process in the
evolving transference–countertransference relationship.

   Bromberg (1996) presents his work with Max, a first-generation
Jewish man who seems overly concerned with pleasing his mother
and is compulsively identified with her idealized view of him as
her contribution to the American intellectual community. Bromberg (1996) states that his view of Max was that he

> was unable to accommodate his mother's image of him into
> an acceptance of himself as a human being with limitations as
> well as assets, and that he continually enacted a dissociated
> self-representation in which he presented himself as the
> "intellectual" who she said he was, while simultaneously
> demonstrating to himself, in every other possible way, that he
> was not who she said he was, and that he was simply a
> "typical American boy doing his own thing."
>
> (p. 521)

> Max and I had been engaged in a struggle around what he
> felt, I think accurately, to be my somewhat unsympathetic
> determination to pry him loose from having to be who his
> mother said he was. He insisted that he was not under his
> mother's spell, and that his tendency to use the wrong words

when he did not really know their meaning, was simply a matter of insufficient familiarity with the dictionary rather than an unconscious loyalty to his bond with his mother. I had been giving him my "favorite" interpretation in different ways for a long time, and he had consistently (but deferentially) rejected this view, politely protesting that he is his own person, that he also loves his mother, and that there is no opposition between the two. I was in the midst of delivering the "truth" once again, when he said to me, in a tone of benevolent exasperation, "I really want to accept what you are saying about me, because I respect you, but I just can't, and I feel caught between ... between ... Sylvia and the chiropodist." I exploded with laughter, and when I calmed down and wiped the tears from my eyes, I looked up apprehensively, expecting him to be hurt, shamed, or angry at my response. He was neither. Max looked genuinely bewildered. So, I explained why I was laughing, and told him what the actual expression (Scylla and Charybdis) was. He replied, hesitantly, "What's that?" and I then told him the myth. I found myself unable to omit a single detail ... When I had finished, he paused, tellingly, and allowed that he was "immensely appreciative" because, as he put it, "you just told me something I needed to know all my life." I was astounded not only that he could let himself use sarcasm with me, but that he could hear it so clearly. I was also shocked (and slightly embarrassed) at having been so unaware of my shift in role.

(p. 523)

This was a critical moment in the treatment for both patient and analyst: it was an enactment of the patient's pathological pattern, both becoming his mother's idealized intellectual son and her differential child. Bromberg's participation in this enactment was clearly spontaneous, reflecting the inevitable transformation of a historic narrative into a repetitive current behavioral pattern. However, because the interpersonal and relational perspectives maintain a view of representation as either verbalizable or not verbalizable, there is little focus on a structural view of countertransference which would include the analyst exploring his/her own unconscious motivation for the enactment. There is some suggestion by the patient that perhaps Bromberg had a need to one-up him, to demonstrate his superior position. However, this is not explored, and the enactment, which is clearly important and helpful, remains an experience-near event and perhaps an important moment in the patient's life and in the narrative of the analysis. The unconscious experience remains an experience-near expansion of the patient's and analyst's awareness of what has transpired between them without any attempts at interpretation or explanation.

I would like to contrast Bromberg's example, which rests more solidly in the interpersonal camp, with one in which there is an evolution the analyst's role representing both a historical and new transference figure (Burke, 1992), reflecting the further development of relational psychoanalysis emphasizing both the inter- and intrasubjective perspectives. Davies (1994) courageously contextualizes her clinical illustration through addressing the question of the erotic transference–countertransference relationship from a new perspective which she describes as post-oedipal sexuality. She (Davies, 1994) believes that the capacity to address this typically frightening erotic configuration within the transference–countertransference relationship is predicated upon the analyst's capacity to sustain and tolerate the complementary and concordant countertransference responses (Racker, 1982) specific to passionate desire in the analytic relationship. This paper highlights important elements in the evolving relational perspective, including an emphasis on self-disclosure and a more egalitarian or symmetrical relationship between patient and analyst in terms of prerogative and power. We see an emphasis on the phenomenology of the clinical interaction as opposed to a structural interpretation of unconscious patterns, motives, or defenses, as multiple aspects of the historical patterns and limits determined by the patient's experience of anxiety are enacted in the transference–countertransference relationship.

Davies describes a moment in her relationship with a long-term analytic patient who had already made great progress but was now cautiously opening up a forbidden aspect of his history and self-system within the analysis. The patient had been sexually abused by his mother's brother, his uncle, who had financially and emotionally replaced the patient's father who had died early in the patient's life. Davies observes that, although many historical and current issues had been addressed in the treatment, sexuality was assiduously avoided until a critical moment in the sixth year of the analysis when:

David unexpectedly and rather accusingly said to me one day, "Forgive me if I'm wrong, but I think you're flirting with me." I was caught off guard as much by the surprising directness of David's expression as by the accuracy of the perception. Indeed, upon reflection, it appeared that my comments and manner were somewhat flirtatious. Was this behavior on my part new, or was David seeing it and calling my attention to it for the first time? The "anti-transference" of analyst as woman seemed to be knocking at our door. The decision about whether or not to let her in hung between us. I was responding to David's sexuality ... he had finally made his way to mine. How to respond?

"I think you're right," I said. "I hadn't been aware of it until you said something, but I was flirting with you."

"You're not supposed to do that, you know," he said, with a decidedly mischievous smile.

"I'm not?" I replied, now knowingly joining the play, which I felt he had initiated.

"Uh, uh," he responded, "you know, three quarters of those books behind you would say that you shouldn't be doing this."

"You're probably right," I answered. "So now you're telling me that I'm not only flirting ... but I'm flirting with the forbidden. Do you think I should stop?"

David smiled engagingly, but his smile turned quickly and deeply sad. He became quiet. I wondered if I had ventured too far. "You're inviting me to play with you," he said. "We've played together in a lot of different places ..." His voice trailed off.

"This one feels much, much scarier," I suggested.

"I can't play here." He shook his head. "We better not go into this place."

"We could close the door on this place," I offered. "It would feel much safer."

"Maybe we'd better," he answered, but he looked so profoundly sad.

"You look so sad. You don't really want to close this door, I think. But you know it's intriguing. We've been to so many really truly terrifying places together, you and I ... the abuse, your reactions to it, your fantasies about it, your mother's depression, her involvement with your uncle. Isn't it interesting that this playful, flirtatious place should feel like the scariest one of all?"

David and Davies are able to work out a safe way to move into this forbidden area of discourse and address and resolve his anxieties around sexuality and his experiences of sexual abuse and abandonment. This psychoanalytic moment can be thought of as a metaphorical enactment in which the analytic dialogue becomes a presentational, dreamlike experience in which analyst and patient are living out, creating, a new experience of trust in the most intimate moments of a relationship.

Davies's example is quite moving and illustrates several important aspects of relational psychoanalysis, including extending the interpersonal view that we are all shaped by the anxiety and disapproval of our early life. However, rather than simply being an attempt to expand the patient's awareness, there is a direct attempt to expand the patient's experience through moments of meeting (B.P.C.S.G. et al., 1998), performative experience which may or may not be brought into verbal representations through interpretation and explanation. Although Davies and most relational analysts do not attend to the form of representation (interpretations), there is often a dramatic, metaphoric, and poetic use of language which maybe associated with the dreamlike primary process language that Freud described in *The Interpretation of Dreams*.

Davies's paper illustrates a core aspect of relational psychoanalysis, questioning and revising many concepts that defined classical psychoanalysis, which typically interprets sexuality as a function of the Oedipus complex as opposed to more complex and mature views of sexuality. Greenberg and Mitchell's (1983) book, which is the cornerstone of relational psychoanalysis, redefined psychoanalytic thought and practice as a two-person, non-drive-centered perspective, which was the beginning of a revolutionary shift in psychoanalysis. In questioning traditional drive theory and particularly allowing for the individual analyst's experience to be a critical part of the change process, they moved psychoanalysis from its metapsychological core focused on interpretation and remembering into a phenomenological, collaborative, highly individualistic, performative approach to the psychoanalytic project.

The questions and uses of self-disclosure have been an important aspect of the development of relational psychoanalysis. The question of self-disclosure is quite complex and often reflects important elements of the analyst's personality and their position in relation to the differential of power in the analytic relationship. Aron (1999) describes two dimensions of self-disclosure as symmetrical and asymmetrical, with symmetry referring to specific aspects of what the analyst and patient are able or willing to reveal to each other, which is modified or limited by the dimension of asymmetry, which has to do with analytic roles, the prerogatives and responsibilities of the patient and analyst. Although Aron is extremely open with his patients about his experience and thoughts, he will restrict some of what he says in order to maintain the role differential, reflecting his decision that some of his experiences and thoughts would not be appropriate for the patient. Renik (1995), another influential relational theorist, presents a more radical view of self-disclosure, presenting his belief that anonymity is an impossible and false ideal, and that the analytic process is one in which we become progressively more able to reveal our thoughts, which can often touch off a great deal of anxiety in the analyst. He (Renik, 1995) cites an important paper by Singer (1971), a second-generation interpersonal analyst, who, against the assumptions of his time, revealed a great deal of personal information; he concluded that this had a positive effect on the treatment, and that many patients suffer from the secrets that were maintained in the family and rarely had an opportunity to be helpful to their parents, stunting their capacity for empathy and creating feelings of inadequacy because of a lack of opportunity to be useful members of the family and their world.

Bass (2015) discusses the impact that Ferenczi's work had on the evolving sense of mutuality in relational psychoanalysis. He particularly places emphasis on the dialogue of the unconscious between the patient and analyst, observing that patients often know a great deal about their analysts but are either reluctant to bring this up or are not fully aware of this unconscious knowledge. Although not advocating mutual analysis, as Ferenczi did, he does highlight the importance of the analyst encouraging and taking seriously their patient's observations and thoughts about the analyst's unconscious issues that inevitably arise in the treatment. This increased clinical emphasis on mutuality highlights the importance of a more egalitarian relationship and the uniqueness of each analytic couple.

Many relational theorists emphasize a shift in the analytic concept of transference which is expanded to include the analyst's participation as a new 'transference' object, performatively expanding the patient's experience from the limitations of their early experience of transference as only representing historical objects. In many ways, this different use of transference as representing a historical object and, alternatively, representing a new object can be thought of as a return to the pragmatic perspective that Sullivan introduced, focusing on growth rather than interpretation and the recovery of repressed memories. Benjamin (2009) highlights an important element in this process of growth, developing the concept of recognition, which highlights an intersubjective, structural focus to both the process of self-disclosure and the expansion of an intersubjective dimension. Recognition and what she describes as the analytic third involve an awareness of how one exists in another's mind. This intersubjective focus, although not specifically using the concept of the unconscious, expands the analytic relationship from a mostly performative or phenomenological focus to focusing on the internal processes of patient and analyst. From a developmental perspective, we can see concepts of recognition and the analytic third as involving processes similar to that of mentalization (Fonagy & Target, 2007), the reflective processes of one mind becoming aware of another's mind.[5] The intersubjective perspective which Benjamin highlights is one of the features that differentiates interpersonal and relational psychoanalysis and, like self-disclosure, is quite attractive to practitioners but creates important issues about the rules to follow as a relational analyst. Unlike classical psychoanalysis, there is no concept like the standard technique (Arlow & Brenner, 1988) which practitioners can learn and feel secure following.

Many of Mitchell's (1990) papers directly address questions of the rules for conducting psychoanalytic treatment and the underlying metapsychological propositions, or how to function as a relational analyst without losing the professional focus of psychoanalytic treatment. Mitchell's writings make clear that he places himself in a strongly egalitarian relationship with his patient and focuses on his subjectivity, his experience in the moment-to-moment interaction between himself and his patient. He questions many of the important metapsychological and structural concepts presented in classical psychoanalysis; questioning the underlying motivational theory of classical psychoanalysis, the drive and libido theory, his paper on "Wishes, Needs and Interpersonal Negotiation" (Mitchell, 1991) focuses on the complexity of the experience of desire and the impossibility of understanding motivation aside from the relational context of the people involved. He begins this paper by making it clear that the traditional imperative of not gratifying the patient's desires and requests is impossible without recognizing the analyst's own subjective state which encompasses many variables. Mitchell accurately describes the rules of classical psychoanalysis:

> The analyst's role in this model of the analytic process is clear: do not gratify. Any misguided efforts to soften the rigors and abstinence of the analytic experience is irresponsible and robs the analysand of the chance to more fully free himself from a seductive embeddedness within infantile fantasies and illusions.
>
> (p. 150)

In rejecting the one-person demand that the analyst not gratify the patient, Mitchell focuses on the two-person, relational situation, stating a more difficult analytic task which is to assess the relational situation in which expressions of wishes, needs, and desires

are constantly changing along with the analytic context in which
the same request may have different meanings at different times.
Aron (1999) illustrates the difficulty of knowing what a particular
request means by describing three fictional supervisors' under-
standings and recommendations to a fictional therapist who presents the same material to each supervisor. Aron points out that
each supervisor has a different understanding of the patient's
request based on their a priori theory and possibly on their
personality. Mitchell (1991) extends this perspective, highlighting the analyst's subjectivity, which may change depending
on factors in the analyst's personal and professional life, and
also raising the question of the fit between patient and analyst.
For Mitchell, the question becomes how the analyst and patient
negotiate their different experiences of the analytic relationship.
Mitchell sees the essential analytic process as an expansion of
both the patient's and the analyst's capacity to reflect on their experience, both in the analytic relationship and in their extra-analytic lives.
Mitchell states:

> Rather than being one in a linear sequence of developmental
> tasks, the negotiation between one's own desires and those of
> others is a lifelong struggle (Stern, 1985). The analyst's
> expertise resides in developing and drawing the patient into a
> collaborative inquiry which allows both the patient's desires
> and the analyst's authentic participation to find a home.
>
> (p. 169)

Mitchell presents his arguments from a phenomenological perspective, perhaps expecting his readers to understand that this
expansion of the capacity to use reflective processes involves a
version of making the unconscious conscious.

In an important illustration of the analytic process from a relational perspective, Mitchell (1990) presents his case of Robert, an
executive who was tortured by self-doubt, fearing that he had
made a mistake at work which would have disastrous consequences. Pretty soon, this narrow concern expanded to include
Robert's intense worries about his wife and children which were
articulated in a dream that the patient reported. Mitchell's

presentation of his patient's complex dream engages traditional analytic material typically identified as "the Royal Road to the Unconscious," which often focuses on repressed elements of the past. However, Mitchell's interpretation of the dream is largely directed at stimulating a self-reflective process, implicitly bringing the focus into the here and now of the analytic relationship. Interestingly, the patient both rejected and affirmed Mitchell's interpretation, presenting another dream which further elaborated his anxiety about his actions causing disasters. I want to quote from Mitchell's paper to illustrate this affective exchange, what Mitchell previously discussed as a process of negotiation – which goes on continuously in psychoanalytic relationships – that many non-relational analysts would define as defensiveness or resistance.

> I told Robert I thought the dream might be understood to suggest that there were places in his mind that he was not aware of, in which pieces of his own experience had been placed for safekeeping and future reference. I also suggested that his struggles with his son were in some measure reflective of struggles with a part of himself that had been long buried. Robert began the next session by complimenting me on my "creative" understanding of the dream, by which it soon became clear he meant far-fetched.

(p. 22)

In this paper, Mitchell is attempting to articulate his view of the analyst's authority which, he believes, resides not in a specialized knowledge of what is in the patient's mind but in a mutual process of organizing the patient's conscious and unconscious experience in one of the many possible ways that would be conducive to a richer and less self-sabotaging existence. From this perspective, the patient would be less likely to disown experience and would become more aware of their own agency and participation, becoming the author of their own life. For Mitchell and other relational analysts, the goal of treatment is to expand the patient's potential life experience and not to have a superior sense of the analyst's or the dyad's truth.

Dimensions of the Unconscious in Interpersonal and Relational Psychoanalysis

Interpersonal and relational psychoanalysts following in Sullivan's footsteps maintain a phenomenological and pragmatic approach, conceiving of the unconscious as reflected in the limitations which circumscribe the patient's life and thoughts. In the authors that were cited, the idea of the unconscious was used more descriptively than structurally, although, in each clinical example, we can see the analysis was focused on expanding and enriching the patient's experience. It would seem that the emphasis is largely on a topographic model, with little attention given to structure, inner dynamics, or different forms of representation. The main structural component focuses on differentiating historic from current internal objects, with the analyst frequently taking the role of the good new object in contrast to the critical and limiting historical object. The emphasis on collaboration, self-disclosure, and power might suggest a different form of structure, an intersubjective rather than an intrasubjective relational structure, or, as Stern (2013) suggests, something more like field theory.

Notes

1 See Helen Swick Perry's (1982) biography of Sullivan, *Psychiatrist of America*.
2 Sullivan's concept of the self-system is very similar to Winnicott's (1971) concept of the false self.
3 See *Interpersonal Psychoanalysis: The Selected Papers of Clara M. Thompson* (Green, 1964).
4 Levenson's (2005) book *The Fallacy of Understanding* develops this argument and is highly recommended.
5 Aron's (2001) book *A Meeting of Minds* develops this theme of the intersubjective experience of psychoanalysis.

Chapter 3

Developmental Perspectives on the Unconscious

Introduction

This chapter focuses on psychoanalytic theories which present developmental models of the mind, highlighting the qualities and structures that develop in an organized pattern, becoming progressively capable of integrating experience in predictable and progressively more mature ways. These developmental theories are inherently two-person models, viewing the child as developing within the context of the family. Winnicott's (1971) well-known statement that "there is no such thing as a baby" was his attempt to highlight that babies always exist in the matrix of a family, more specifically connected to a mother or caretaker. Although these developmental theories typically present a phenomenological, experience-near clinical approach, they also present a structural approach to the mind in which underlying structures determine the individual's perception and ability to act in the world. I want to highlight the idea that these developmental theories incorporate both phenomenological and structural perspectives. Like the interpersonal and relational theories presented in the previous chapter, the concept of the unconscious is rarely used as a structural concept, but is described as a quality of thought, as something outside awareness, similar to Freud's topographic model. These developmental theories have implicit and explicit structural elements suggesting a structural unconscious, often elaborating and utilizing concepts derived from neuropsychology and cognitive science.

DOI: 10.4324/9781003058274-4

Developmental theories, in contrast to the interpersonal and relational or Freudian theories, focus on the growth of the mind as an internal structure, conceiving of psychopathology as a result of failures in early caretaking experiences rather than as a result of trauma or the internalization of toxic parental experience. Because of this perspective, the analyst's task is not simply to provide an experience with a new, less toxic object but to stimulate the development of the patient's mental capacity, enabling the subject to generate experience and utilize new modes of thought; we may think of this process as the creation of mind (Symington, 2007). Referring back to the previous discussion of the dimensions of the unconscious, these developmental theories focus on how inner and external experiences are represented in the mind and the mind as having multiple modes of representing experience. The primary theorists who will be discussed in this chapter are Kohut, Winnicott, and Fonagy. As background to discussing these psychoanalytic theorists, I will briefly highlight some of Piaget's and Bowlby's contributions, which preceded the psychoanalytic developmental theorists and were part of a general base of knowledge that undoubtedly contributed to their and our understanding of child development.

Freud introduced the concept of structure in psychoanalysis, describing a hierarchical, tripartite division of the mind in which the ego, superego, and id, or the CNS, PCS and UCS, formed distinct structures; these were regulated by internal forces or dynamics, including repression and the pleasure principle, which defined and limited the relationships between these structures and resulted in behavioral and cognitive experiences that required the analyst to understand how his/her interventions affected the different structures and forces in the mind and the resulting behavior, thought, and speech. Freud's development of the structural approach was well ahead of many of his peers, who approached patients' psychological problems from a descriptive and prescriptive perspective. The formal concept of structuralism as an approach to understanding human behavior and culture developed in the early twentieth century and, like Freud's ideas, attempted to look beyond the explicit phenomena to the structures and rules or algorithms which underlay the events that were observed.

Roman Jakobson, a Russian functional linguist, was a critical figure in the expansion of structuralism to the social sciences, including developmental psychology and psychoanalysis. Piaget (1973) is often considered to be part of the structuralist movement, and his work illuminated the mental structures that allowed children to learn about the world. He believed that children's capacity to learn evolved in an organized way through several stages which were dependent on an environment that could match itself to the stage that the child was in. He described four major stages, each of which had several substages which defined the child's capacity to learn and know about the world. The stages that Piaget described were: the sensorimotor stage, the pre-operational stage, the concrete operational stage, and the formal operational stage. He described schemas or structures[1] which provide mental frameworks that allow the child to interpret and respond to experiences in the environment and are determined or limited by the stage that the child is able to use in apprehending the world. We can think of these schemas as internal structures which organize the child's or individual's understanding, organization, comprehension, and interaction with the world.

Bowlby (1999 [1969]) developed a structural view of the mind which he described as internal working models, schemas that represent highly consistent modes of attachment that an individual develops early in life and that continue to organize the way he/she forms and organizes relationships. Bowlby thought that we each develop an internal working model of the self and an internal working model of others. The internal working model of the self incorporates qualities of self-confidence, self-judgment, and dependency, while the internal working model of others determines patterns of relationship involving connection and avoidance. Bowlby and his associate Mary Ainsworth defined several attachment patterns which have been found to remain highly consistent throughout life: secure attachment, anxious-ambivalent attachment, anxious-avoidant and dismissive-avoidant attachment, and disorganized/disoriented attachment. For Bowlby and others, working models are unconscious structures which organize experience in relationships, perceptions, and emotional responses which are relatively fixed and not a transient set of reactions to moment-to-moment changes in the environment. Bowlby's and Piaget's theories can be thought of as an important background that influenced the psychoanalytic developmental theorists and their views of the unconscious as a developing structure.

Kohut

Kohut (1971, 1984) spent most of his career deeply committed to and involved in classical psychoanalysis, but he eventually became dissatisfied, noting that it did not adequately conceptualize contemporary patients' and therapists' experiences or provide an effective treatment paradigm for contemporary patients suffering from narcissistic disorders.[2] Unlike other theorists who focus on developmental issues, expanding the current models of psychoanalysis, Kohut set out to develop a new psychoanalytic theory, self psychology, through which he could address differences between classical psychoanalysis's archetype of the 'guilty man' and his view of 'tragic man' as the contemporary individual. The difference between the guilty man, who suffered from thoughts, fantasies, and guilt over Oedipal desire, and the tragic man,[3] who finds himself thrown into circumstances outside the possibility of control, is central to both self psychology and many other contemporary theories. Self psychology is a radical two-person theory focused on the emotional development of the individual. Kohut purposely avoided using traditional structural concepts, developing the more experience-near, albeit ambiguous, concept of the self as central to his theory and clinical work. Kohut (1984) believed that the self was part of an innate structure which regulates the development of self-esteem or narcissism as a separate developmental line from the Oedipal trajectory of object love, and that psychopathology was based on failures in the development of the self and the capacity to regulate self-esteem.

The self has two developmental lines which grow from immature to mature organizations: the grandiose self, which has the potential to grow into mature ambitions if the parent or therapist is able to empathically mirror the subject's experience, and the omnipotent or idealized object, which has the potential to develop into mature ideals if the parent or therapist is able to manage experiences of idealization and provide the calming experiences of identification. For Kohut, the development of these structures is dependent on the capacity of the other, the parent or therapist, to provide an empathic response to the individual's needs. For Kohut (1984), the analyst is not simply a kinder, more gentle person; he thought of the analyst as a self-object, describing a function involving the ability to focus on understanding the individual's subjective experience and respond empathically to the subject's needs for mirroring and idealization. Kohut's concept of self-object describes a particular structural aspect of a two-person relationship which is not mutual or symmetrical but is one in which the parent or therapist, the self-object, is completely focused on the other's needs, perceptions, and experience. Kohut is suggesting a complete focus on the patient's or child's self and consistently rejects introducing an objective or positivist perspective of external reality into this intersubjective relationship. In conceiving of the intersubjective analytic relationship as a self–self-object relationship, Kohut (1984) cogently states how rare it is for an individual to be the complete center of another's attention, empathy, and interest for even as short a time as the 45 minutes of an analytic session.

Kohut illustrates this empathic perspective and presents a case which challenges many of the rules of classical psychoanalysis, particularly the concept that the patient is expressing infantile, immature wishes in which they demand to have their needs gratified, while the analyst's task is to introduce a sense of reality into this system and not gratify the patient's infantile demands. Kohut describes the following situation with his patient, a university professor, who wanted to begin analysis but asked the analyst to forgo his fees for a somewhat lengthy period so that the professor could purchase a vacation home in a Colorado ski resort. Not only is Kohut challenging the essential Oedipal narrative of entitlement, but he is also challenging related issues around the psychoanalytic frame and the importance of the patient paying for therapy. It is interesting to me that Kohut presents this case without reference to the issue of the challenge to the rules of psychoanalytic practice that are an important aspect of the psychoanalytic canon. Kohut responds to the patient in a very empathic way, disclosing that, as far as he is concerned, he can afford to wait for his fee[4] but that, as they proceed in the analysis, they may find that this request has meanings that go beyond the patient's wish to simply invest in this vacation property. Kohut maintains his empathic perspective, viewing this situation from the subjective perspective of the patient rather than from an a priori view that the patient is attempting to get away with something or not respecting the analyst's position or financial needs. Although Kohut presents this situation as if it is a simple negotiation, it is a truly profound illustration of the potential difficulty maintaining the empathic self–self-object relationship that he believes is the necessary intersubjective structure of self psychology.

Although Kohut does not describe a particular structure equivalent to the dynamic unconscious, he seems to develop an interesting version of the topographic model in which a person is able to be engaged in a series of actions, without self-awareness, which often cause the subject pain and difficulty. Kohut (1971) refers to these actions and thoughts as archaic self–self-object relations, action without reflective thought that is designed to get certain unpleasant reactions, which, in analysis, may become transformed into mature self-object relations in which the individual is able to consciously understand and regulate their own affective experience and negotiate a more satisfactory self–self-object relationship. It is the movement from a lack of awareness to the capacity for self-awareness that seems central to Kohut's work and his understanding of the effects of unconscious processes on behavior.

Beebe and Lachmann (2020) are among many psychoanalysts who have extend Kohut's ideas through their research on implicit forms of communication between mothers and infants and patients and therapists. Their work can be understood as elaborating Kohut's concept of empathy and the development of self-esteem. In Beebe's (2005) research on mother–infant interaction, one immediately sees the effect of the parent's un-empathic and indifferent response to the baby, which often involves literally turning away from the child, compared with the parent's rapt, empathic attention and approving smiles. Beebe and Lachmann (2020) developed the idea of scripts, a way of thinking about schemas that emphasizes the two-person structure of self–self-object relations implicit in Kohut's theory of the unconscious and highlights that the individual subject is continuously finding self-objects to join in replaying their self–self-object structure, even when the results are painful and punishing.

The question why we would recreate painful experiences has been a critical question that psychoanalysis has struggled with on both abstract[5] and pragmatic levels. Kohut's (1979, 1984) perspective on this persistent question involves a radical two-person view of the overwhelming need for self-objects throughout life, our need to have our existence empathically reflected (mirrored) without which we would become completely fragmented, isolated, and lost in an endless, timeless, formless experience, like a black hole in space. Kohut argues that the most fundamental experience of anxiety is not castration anxiety but disintegration anxiety, involving the self losing a sense of internal cohesion and simultaneous connection with other self-objects in the world. He believes that the need for self-objects is like a need for psychological oxygen without which the individual will be emotionally dead. Another way of understanding Kohut's position is that the need for self–self-object relations is based on unconscious (implicit) schemas which may result in apparently unhealthy modes of being involving archaic self-object relations that result in painful experiences; these, however, essentially maintain self-cohesion at the cost of potentially more mature ambitions and ideals. We may think of addictions and abusive relationships as extreme examples of archaic self–self-object relations which are difficult to change because they maintain archaic self–self-object relationships.

The critical elements in self psychology's formulation of unconscious experience involve the development of schemas (Wolf et al., 2001) which are not mediated by language but are organized around implicit affective experiences. Stern's (1985) work on the psychological birth of the human infant presents an argument that is similar to Kohut's, describing the intersubjective development of internal representations of self and other like Kohut's concept of self–self-object relations. Stern (1992) connected psychoanalytic concepts of unconscious fantasy with the development of the capacity to transform experience into thought, integrating contemporary cognitive and developmental findings into the concept of "pre-narrative envelopes," narrative structures, like scripts, which emerge from the infant's intersubjective interactions and ongoing motivational states. Stern describes the pre-narrative envelope as the building blocks of thought which synthesize the flood of internal and external sensations and perception that the infant experiences. Stern (1992) states:

> the mind appears to process, in parallel and in partial independence, a large number of simultaneous mental happenings. During an experience, instinctual urgings, visual images, affect shifts, sensations, motor actions, ideas, states of arousal, language, place and space, time, etc., are all processed simultaneously in parallel throughout all 'centres' in the mind as well as in specialized ones devoted to processing each ('Parallel Distributed Processing' (PDP)). The parallel processing of each element is carried out with lower-level, local, mental operations which are never translatable into subjective experience. These mental processes are operationally unconscious. This results in a sort of mental pandemonium of mental action in multiple 'centres' ('modules'): many characters in search of an author. This is the normal state of things. And from the interplay, co-ordination, integration of these lower-level processes, a more global mental event emerges: 'an emergent property' of the mind, which has coherence and sense in the context in which it emerged. That is to say, the diverse events and feelings are tied together as necessary elements of a single unified happening which assumes a narrative-like structure. The 'pre-narrative envelope' is just such an emergent property of mind that accomplishes this integration of experience.

(p. 295)

Stern believes that these early processes of creating meaning, mental construction, or thinking utilize the infant's hard-wired capacity for pattern recognition, generalization, coherence, and awareness of intentionality and temporality which create schemas that organize the infant's action. Although not verbal, pre-narrative envelopes are organized around early experiences involving dramatic lines: plots which unfold along a temporal gradient. Stern (1992, p. 314) states that the pre-narrative envelope is:

> the unit of experience from which later true autobiographical narrative acts of meaning are created. In this sense, it implies a discoverable order between the two, and views the hermeneutic approach as complementary. From a clinical point of view, thinking in terms of 'pre-narrative envelopes' provides an additional search-strategy for the origins of the patient's representational world. It puts a greater emphasis on the detailed exploration of repeated 'micro-interactions' in both past and present.

Winnicott

Winnicott began his career as a pediatrician, bringing his experience with mothers and infants to his psychoanalytic understanding of the development of mind. Winnicott (1971; Newirth 2003; Grosskurth, 1986) identified himself as a Kleinian while also expanding Kleinian theory through addressing the importance of the external world. Winnicott did not explicitly conceptualize the unconscious as a structure, preferring to write from an experience-near, phenomenological perspective. However, his emphasis on the importance of illusion, transitional experience, and play expanded our understanding of the unconscious as a potentially creative structure beyond Freud's view of the unconscious as a seething cauldron of sexual and aggressive drives, infantile wishes expressed in symptoms, dreams, and humor. For Freud, dreams and symptoms were an encoded message which required translation in order to arrive at the unconscious meaning. Winnicott viewed the unconscious as a developing structure which is interdependent on experiences with an other, parent or analyst, who would be able to enter into what he later described as play. There are two dimensions to Winnicott's implicit ideas about the unconscious: first, that it is a separate and parallel organization to consciousness; and second, that it is the source of vitality, energy, and the quality of feeling fully alive. Claire Winnicott (Winnicott et al., 1989) described a poem that she found in one of Winnicott's notebooks after he died in which he described his concept of the unconscious as a life-giving center of energy, power, and aliveness, using the imagery of a tree which can feed on an infinite source of life and be "evergreen."

This poem, "Sleep," illustrates Winnicott's view of the unconscious as a structure which provides the possibility of being fully alive as a psychological being. We can contrast the experience of being fully alive with the sense of being dead, numb, and simply going through the motions of living (Green, 1993), in zombie-like states of doing what one is programmed to do, what is expected. Winnicott elaborates this idea further, identifying a dual structure of the self which he initially described as the true self and false self and later, I think in a more meaningful way, the self as a subject and the self as an object. For Winnicott, this is not a version of the topographic model of the presence and absence of awareness. For Winnicott, these organizations of self serve different purposes and have different characteristics, more like Freud's structural model; the self as an object is focused on the external world and is largely pragmatic, while the self as a subject is largely focused on the inner world, creating personal meaning, often within intimate relationships. Winnicott begins his developmental theory with a radical two-person conceptualization, one focused on the intersubjective relationship, stating that there is no such thing as a baby and insisting that we need to understand that the baby always exists within an immediate relationship with the mother and within the wider context of the family and culture.[6]

Winnicott challenges the positivist orientation of the one-person perspective in psychoanalysis, emphasizing the importance of the mother fostering the development of illusion (Winnicott, 1971) in the child before tackling the second task of disillusioning the child. Winnicott (1971) expands his idea of the importance of developing the capacity for illusion, suggesting that the mother and family should be able to join the child in the development of transitional experiences, including special objects (dolls, toys) which provide the child with the opportunity for creating meaning in the world as opposed to having to accept the meanings that have been imposed by outside authorities. Winnicott describes these transitional objects and experiences as the first "not me" experiences which allow the child to begin to develop meaning in and for the family, developing a sense of power, agency, and control. Consider a family that is about to leave for home after visiting relatives, and the child is unable to find his/her special toy. All of the adults immediately take on the urgent task of looking for the special toy, the transitional object, often calling it by name and accepting its affective role in the child's mind and the family's emotional life. These are delicate moments in a child's development, moments when the child is able to create the emotional world of the family, as opposed to having the rules of external reality imposed on him/her, crushing this early sense of the power of his/her mind to influence and create experiences in the world. In plain language, Winnicott is presenting the importance of play in psychological well-being; however, he takes the radical step of suggesting that play is not a trivial or childish activity, and that psychotherapy and psychoanalysis are forms of play which facilitate the development of the unconscious mind and, as he suggests in his poem, are the source of aliveness and vitality.

Winnicott's writing style is phenomenological, experience-near, conversational, and optimistic, which contrasts with the more abstract, metapsychological, and theoretical style of his predecessors and mentor Melanie Klein (Grosskurth, 1986). For example, he restates Klein's concepts of the child's greed and aggression, describing them as ruthlessness, with the implication that it is a step on the way towards compassion (ruth) and restating Klein's depressive position as that of the position of concern, of becoming aware of the other in a more complex, multi-dimensional, empathic way. I have often thought that these linguistic differences reflected important differences in each theorist's family and cultural background and also highlight aspects of the history of psychoanalysis in which Klein was introducing a more psychological and less biological approach to the mind, what we think of now as intersubjective, while Winnicott, because of many other contemporary analytic writers, was able to develop a radical two-person position without the need to justify his thinking.

Winnicott presents an interesting structural view of the unconscious as a form of creativity, spontaneity, and, although he does not use this word, passion. Winnicott's initial formulation of the structure of the mind described the false self as involving the experience of being negated and forced to conform to the other's beliefs or the demands of cultural roles, and the true self reflecting the child's experience of having their creative efforts responded to by their parents. Prior to his death, Winnicott revised this theory, describing these two parallel structures as being those of a subject and of an object. This change in language involved a recognition that we all have to conform to the expectation of parents, family, and culture, and that experience is different from being a subject, where our capacity to create meaning in relationships and in other mediums is in the foreground. Winnicott further differentiates what he calls object relating from object usage and presents an interesting thesis in which object relating involves the person treating the other and the world as instances of prior expectations, and historical experiences as transference objects. Object usage requires the person to place the other and the world outside his/ her omnipotent control, to destroy prior expectations, and to be able to experience the other and the world as separate objects who need to be recognized as equal subjects, which would seem to reflect his concept of the position of concern. In spite of his warm personal style, Winnicott does not advocate a symmetrical and mutual analytic relationship but suggests that the analyst, like a parent, has different responsibilities and ways of being than the patient or child. He points to the importance of time as a dimension in the growth of children and patients and suggests that it is a sign of maturity, the development of the capacity for object usage, when the child or patient can recognize the sacrifices that the parent or therapist has made for them.

Unfortunately, Winnicott did not present many clinical examples of his work, reflecting his reluctance to impose his vision and idiom on others, but preferred that clinicians find their own language and voice. His colleague, collaborator, and analysand Masud Khan helped him organize his writing, and Khan's (1974, 2019) own clinical work presented many illustrations of how Winnicott's theories are applied to psychoanalysis. In a very interesting paper, Khan (1974) presents the case of a woman who he sees as illustrating two of Winnicott's (1971) ideas: that we all contain a male and female part, and that we are split as both objects and subjects. As an object, Khan believed that this patient identified herself as a woman with little agency who was compelled to respond to others' desires. However, as he continued to work with her, he came to see that there was another aspect to her life, that of being a subject, which was identified with a male self which held sway when she was being creative. This patient did not seem to have the two aspects of her self integrated nor was she even able to be aware of each as separate dimensions of herself. In our current conceptual language, the patient's two self-states were dissociated from each other. Khan emphasizes the difference between the patient's self as being an object, in which the patient felt that she had to just go along with others' expectations, often for sexual contact where the patient felt affectively numb, and the patient's self as a subject in her work as an artist, where she felt fully alive, agentic, and in control. It would seem that, for Khan and Winnicott, the self as an object related passively to the external world, while the self as a subject represented the creative potential of her inner world, her unconscious, which created meaning and a world that was hers, in which she was the author. Winnicott's idea of being a subject extends his idea of the creative potential of transitional experiences and the place where we live.

Fonagy

Peter Fonagy (1995, 2008; Fonagy & Target, 2007) is a contemporary British psychologist and psychoanalyst who has integrated cognitive research, attachment theory, and therapy. His work describes two parallel modes of organizing, representing, and generating experience which can develop into a third more mature mode. These structures of experience are the mode of psychic equivalence, the pretend mode, and mentalization. The mode of psychic equivalence occurs when the child or individual assumes that what is in their mind is the same as what is in the other person's mind and also represents reality. We can see that this mode of representing experience can be extremely literal, concrete, or absolute, reflecting a view that external reality is fixed and cannot be altered, a world of absolute facts. The pretend mode of experience is quite different and involves the child or adult being able to imagine alternatives and play with representations of inner and outer reality. The pretend mode can be thought of as similar to Winnicott's concept of transitional experience. Fonagy and Target (2007) illustrate these two modes of representation with the following example: a little boy, in the pretend mode, has turned a chair on its side and is playing that it is a tank when his father comes into the room and asks, is this a chair or a tank? The child immediately turns the chair upright and leaves the room. It is unfortunate that the father could not join the child in his play, continuing to develop the imaginary theme of playing at war, playing with aggression, as opposed to having to define the chair in the psychic equivalence mode through asking the question: "what is it?" Fonagy and Target (2007) make it clear that, in situations like this, the parent needs to be able to respond in a 'marked' way indicating that both he and the child know they are playing with reality and that it is a separate experience from that of objective reality. In many ways, this example can be thought of as highlighting similarities between the different developmental psychoanalytic theorists; marked communication can also be seen as a form of empathic mirroring and a form of creating transitional experiences.[7]

The third mode of representation, which Fonagy describes as mentalization, is where the child or adult is able to reflect on what is in his/her mind and also what is in the other's mind while understanding that these thoughts are not facts, but represent an imaginative view which can be checked out through conversation and observation. One aspect of the capacity for mentalization involves the child learning to enter the pretend mode with others, through which the child learns that important aspects of intersubjective reality can be created with others, that intersubjective aspects of experience require involvement with reliable others. Fonagy (2014) and his colleagues emphasize the importance of a somewhat secure attachment as necessary for the development of the capacity for mentalization and locate individuals who are diagnosed with borderline personality disorders as lacking in the capacity for mentalization, even though they are often able to enter the pretend mode when alone, creating a personal alternative universe.

Fonagy includes references to the unconscious in his writing, often describing these unconscious experiences as events which have never been empathically marked by a parent. In a most interesting discussion of this failure, when the parent is unable to use marked speech and gestures to reflect (mirror) the simultaneous reality and non-reality of an experience, but reflects it in a flat way, the child internalizes this experience within the mode of psychic equivalence as an alien internal object, like a ghost that lives within the subject and is experienced as a torturous internal object. It would seem that, for Fonagy, the capacity to mentalize, to self-reflect and represent experience as possible, is equivalent to Winnicott's concept of a creative unconscious and Kohut's concept of the mature person's ability to empathize with the other. Again, in these developmental theories, the unconscious is seen as a potentially creative way to transform experiences, to become more alive.

Notes

1 The terms schemas and structures are often used interchangeably to indicate what we might think of today as algorithms, organized systems of apprehending, analyzing, and generating meaning.

2 For Kohut, narcissism was a normal developmental line involving the capacity to regulate self-esteem. He published a case study, "The Two Analyses of Mr. Z" (1979), which is thought to be autobiographical, in which he described how he felt that working from a classical perspective was not helpful and working from a self-psychological perspective corrected the deficits of his earlier work with Mr. Z.

3 Kohut and his family were Jewish and left Germany to escape Hitler's persecution. Like the existentialists who emerged after WWII, the sense of tragedy and the impact of culture and history on the individual was quite profound.

4 This would be an example of an idealizing self–self-object transference in which the analyst, like a strong parent, is able to empathically contain the patient's desires in a curious and non-judgmental way.

5 Freud's (1920) development of the repetition compulsion was an attempt to answer this question which caused him to move away from his simpler model of the pleasure-pain principle.

6 Winnicott's consultations with children always included his awareness of the wider family and cultural matrix that the child and mother were located in.

7 Winnicott's (1975) development of the Squiggle Game would be another illustration of being in the pretend mode and the mutual creation of meaning.

Chapter 4

Kleinian Perspectives on the Unconscious

Introduction

Klein can be considered the second most influential theorist after Freud. Although not explicitly critical of Freud's one-person, bio-logical perspective, she implicitly refocused psychoanalysis as a two-person, psychological system (Ogden, 1992), emphasizing the creation of meaning rather than the discharge of energy and the necessity to adapt to the demands of the reality principle.[1] Like Freud, Klein and those theorists who continued the development of 'Kleinian' theory emphasized a structural perspective in which the unconscious is the central structure organizing both intra-subjective and intersubjective psychological processes.

Klein's (1931) early work with children led her to develop the concept of an epistemophilic instinct – the desire to know in which curiosity was a critical motivational structure and which, like other instincts or drives, could be disrupted and repressed in a child's development resulting in inhibitions and symptoms of the inability to learn and be curious. Conceptualizing the desire to know as an instinct or drive reflected one of Klein's important contributions, bridging the Freudian positivist perspective and a contemporary hermeneutic approach which emphasizes the devel-opment of meaning. This movement away from traditional drive theory is reflected in Klein's concept of phantasy as the basic building block of the unconscious. Klein's (1975) concept of phantasy is a complex representational concept, like Stern's (1992) concept of pre-narrative envelopes, which views the mind as

DOI: 10.4324/9781003058274-5

organized around creating narrative meaning which perceives and generates experiences in the world. Early arguments against Klein's concept of phantasy questioned how an infant can make meaning and have phantasies before the advent of language. These arguments thought of the infant as a simple organism unable to think without verbal language, which was thought necessary to encode memories of conscious, reality-based events and has recently been found not to be true neurophysiologically.[2]

Klein's concept of phantasy described several dynamic processes forming the unconscious representational system. She believed that the first psychological event which allowed a child to represent his/her experience involved splitting, in which the infant was able to separate painful from joyful experiences. Splitting allowed the infant to separate and then assign a location to experience; through projective identification, the child was able to locate experiences of pain and joy in either him/herself or in the parent as the location of this experience. Klein describes this process as projective identification in which, unlike a one-person process of attribution, the other – the parent or analyst – experiences the affective experience that the child or patient is evacuating. Experiences of projective identification are not necessarily mediated by language or self-reflective awareness and may occur as an affective or somatic state[3] that can either be immediately re-projected or tolerated and worked with. If we imagine that the infant was able to form a non-verbal phantasy around affective experiences of pain (or joy), often reflected in the child's facial and bodily experience, then the child may feel that the parent is either causing the pain or joy or, through identification, experiencing and containing the pain or joy as a subjective experience which can become thought about and expressed to the child in a marked (Fonagy, 1995) form, naming the feeling and experience. As these experiences become repeated, a concept forms of the early parent as a split internal object (phantasy), which Klein thought of as the good breast that brings pleasure or the bad breast that brings pain. These phantasies, like pre-narrative envelopes (Stern, 1992), are the first representational (cognitive) experiences, a first attempt to map the experiential world in a system of unconscious schemas which organize the individual's mode of apprehending, organizing, and generating experience as an active process of meaning making.

Hana Segal (1978), one of Klein's early collaborators, focused on the development of symbolization, how meaning is created in both the paranoid schizoid and depressive positions. She conceptualized the representational processes in the paranoid schizoid and depressive positions as different forms of symbolization, the former as concrete thought processes and the latter as true symbols. She illustrates this by comparing a psychotic and a non-psychotic person's use of the symbol of a violin, which can represent the penis and sexuality. Whenever I think of this example, the phrase "fiddling around" comes to my mind.

> A patient in mental hospital says he cannot play the violin because he won't masturbate in public. Another patient plays the violin and his material makes it clear that to him, too, the violin represents the penis.
>
> What is the difference in the symbolism? In my paper I made the suggestion that symbol formation develops gradually from paranoid-schizoid to a depressive level of functioning. When symbols are formed by projective identification (in the paranoid schizoid position), the result is what I called a symbolic equation. A part of the ego becomes identified with the subject (the violin) and as a consequence, the symbol is equated with the thing symbolized. The symbol does not represent the object, but is treated as though it was the object. Playing the violin is felt to be masturbation. In the depressive position the object is given up and mourned and the symbol is set up in the inner world – an internal object to begin with, representing the object, but not to be equated with it. The symbolic equation is used to deny the separateness between the subject and the object.[4] The symbol is used to overcome an accepted loss. At moments of regression, symbolism may revert to a concrete form even in non-psychotic individuals.
>
> (p. 316)

Segal (1978) further differentiated the symbolic process in the paranoid schizoid and the depressive positions, describing concrete thought, symbolic equations, in the paranoid schizoid position 'as if' an idea, a symbol, is experienced as the object, as a real object in the external world; in the depressive position, the symbol is thought of as representing many possible meanings, experiencing the symbol from the perspective of 'what if' where the symbol and object are separate and represent many different possibilities. It is important to recognize that, for Segal and other Kleinian theorists, the paranoid schizoid and depressive positions represent a dialectical structure of the unconscious, and that, although these unconscious processes may be expressed in words and actions, their meaning remains formed within unconscious phantasies or structures.

Bion

Klein conceptualized mental structure not as a hierarchical organization but as a dialectical structure involving two forms of apprehending, organizing, and generating experience, the paranoid schizoid and depressive positions, which, unlike traditional libidinal stages, continued to develop throughout life as the individual became more mature and involved in more complex intersubjective relationships. Bion (1959/2013), elaborating the relationship between the paranoid schizoid and depressive positions, drew a double-ended arrow, ↔, in order to emphasize the importance of the dialectical movement between these two representational organizations which contribute to both psychopathology and creativity.

Bion (1970, 2013) expanded Klein's concept of symbolization into a radical two-person conceptualization of the unconscious as a structure of meaning making in which the paranoid schizoid and depressive positions create different forms of meaning and experience. He (Bion, 1965) thought of this as a transformational system in which the raw data of experience, perceptions, affects, and somatic, kinesthetic, and other forms of experiential bits (beta elements) were transformed into meaningful ideas (alpha elements) through a process which he described as the alpha function or the container contained. The container contained refers to both an intrasubjective and an intersubjective process of creating meaning in which the container is the process of thinking and creating meaning, and the contained are the forms of data that thinking utilizes and generates.[5]

Bion believed that projective identification was a normal form of emotional communication which may become pathological if the subject compulsively evacuates all inner contents and does not have the intersubjective experience of his/her projective identifications being contained and elaborated by an other. In non-pathological experience, the infant or patient uses projective identification to rid the self of a painful experience, and the parent or therapist identifies with, emotionally elaborates, and contextualizes the projected experience, transforming it, through processes of reverie, into a meaningful and less frightening experience. Alternatively, if the parent or therapist becomes reactive, feeling threatened by the child or patient's projection, and is unable to contain and transform these emotional beta elements, the experience remains in a concrete paranoid mode, in which each member of the dyad blames the other for making them feel bad, believing that they are good and the other bad in an endless game of hot potato. When the parent or therapist is unable to identify with the patient's disowned experience and becomes frightened or blames the child or patient for being bad, the experience remains in the paranoid schizoid mode and is not transformed into a depressive experience of creating meaning but continues to exist in a paranoid schizoid mode as an absolute fact.

The container contained model is a metaphoric abstraction, shorthand for a very complex clinical process in which transference and countertransference experiences become merged, and the therapist needs to have a highly developed capacity for symbolic, self-reflective thought in order to understand his/her complex unconscious responses to the patient's projective identifications. Schoenhals (1995) describes this process as the analyst's recognition that he/she becomes the patient's (bad) inner object and, regardless of the analyst's intentions or meanings, he/she needs to acknowledge that he/she is the patient's inner object and interpret that to the patient. This process involves a high degree of self-reflection and an ability to transform the concrete emotional aspects of the paranoid schizoid experience into symbolic experiences through processes of reverie and interpretation based on the immediacy of the analytic relationship, as opposed to interpretations which refocus the here-and-now process on to the patient's past history.

In the following example, Schoenhals (1995) describes her process of understanding how she became the patient's inner object through projective identification and became able to understand her attempts to force the patient to conform to her wishes when, previously, both patient and analyst experienced themselves as persecuted by the other. In this example and in other experiences of projective identification, the initial experience is outside the patient's and analyst's awareness, and the disowned inner object is treated as if it is a fact, a concrete thought organized in the paranoid schizoid mode of experience. Schoenhals presents the following clinical vignette in which she became the patient's disowned inner object, the dominating maternal presence, without realizing that she had lost her analytic perspective. It is important to note that, in the following clinical illustration, Schoenhals does not present a historical interpretation but maintains a focus on the here-and-now moment and her part in the analytic dramatic moment.

A patient of mine suddenly announced in her Friday session that she had decided to reduce the frequency of our hours from four to two sessions a week. If I did not agree to this, she would have to quit. I knew she meant it. Again and again during that weekend, I felt distressed by the fact that I was not finding a way to deal with my patient's ultimatum that would allow us to continue with the analysis in the setting it had been up until now, which I was convinced was the only effective way it could continue and also that she needed it ...

Mulling over the events of the Friday session and remembering how my patient had made me feel, I suddenly saw and felt myself to be someone who was force-feeding her with my convictions. The talk with my colleague helped to provide me with a kind of third object so that I could distance myself from being I-O [inner object] – the force-feeding object – far enough to be able to think about it. One of the main reasons my patient had given for reducing the hours had been her financial difficulties, which did not seem to be dire, but were being used – I felt – as an excuse not to discover the real reasons for the reduction. I now took her justification seriously and worked out a plan that I could offer her as a way of continuing the four sessions at a reduced fee for a limited period of time. I felt much more relaxed in my attitude toward the patient when Monday came. During that session, I was able to interpret to her how I thought she felt I was force-feeding her with my judgment about what was good for her and that the only way she felt she could deal with this was to refuse me by saying, no, she did not want four spoonfuls, she only wanted two a week. She felt understood and very relieved by this interpretation, and we were able to work together in an intensely meaningful way for the rest of the hour and throughout that week.

Simply viewing Schoenhals's response as a countertransference reaction to the patient misses two important points. The first is that both patient and analyst were struggling with paranoid schizoid issues of power and control (Newirth, 2003), and both participants experienced this moment concretely as an absolute fact as opposed to seeing the complex possibilities, what Segal refers to as the 'what if' form of thinking in the depressive position. Schoenhals's interpretation highlights the here-and-now quality of Kleinian interpretation (Joseph, 1985) in which the analytic moment is treated as the central experience, without referring to or translating this experience into a historic or genetic explanation. Schoenhals's use of the feeding metaphor brings us into a more dreamlike, poetic moment of a child asserting his/her independence with a dominating maternal presence. This interpretation reflects an unconscious schema, which I imagine is central to this patient's world, whether it actually occurred in her development or not.

The concepts of the container contained and projective identification are difficult to grasp because they reflect complex, multidimensional unconscious processes in both patient and analyst or child and parent. In moments when the patient or child is projecting painful affective experiences, the analyst or parent needs to be able to use processes of reverie to tolerate the discomfort, become curious about his/her experience of discomfort, and affectively and often associatively elaborate these experiences through creating meaning that can be used in an interpretation. This process of 'reverie' may occur very quickly for some patient–analyst dyads, and for others it may take longer, as it did with Schoenhals.

It is important to recognize that projective identification and the process of the container contained are unconscious processes in which the analyst may only be aware of an initial feeling such as being distracted, and that he/she is being a bad analyst by not paying attention to the analytic situation and often attempts to dismiss or resist awareness of the distracting thoughts or actions. Only when the analyst is able to be sufficiently non-judgmental and curious about the distraction and approach it from a 'what if' attitude is it possible to generate symbolic meanings of the 'distraction' and provide a meaningful and evocative interpretation of this experience of projective identification, joining the patient in symbolizing a previous persecutory phantasy.

Ogden (1994, 1995) has a rare ability to articulate his experiences of the container contained and his evolving reverie which highlight the complexity of the container contained process of bringing unconscious phantasies from paranoid schizoid states of concrete action and belief to the symbolic experience of the depressive position, where they can be used in creating a meaningful narrative rather than an endless cycle of repetition and reactivity. In the following example, Ogden (1995) presents a case in which he slowly became aware of the possible meanings embedded in his distracted experience and his reverie functioning as a container for a patient who was unable to create meaning for herself. Although Ogden does not use Kleinian terms such as projective identification, attacks on linking, or reverie in this paper, he presents in a striking and courageous way the phenomenology of these experiences with a patient.

> I found that I experienced increasingly less curiosity about the patient, which absence had quite a disturbing effect on me. It felt equivalent to losing the use of my mind. I experienced a form of claustrophobia during the hours and on occasion defended against this anxiety by obsessionally counting the

minutes until the hour would be over. At other times, I fantasized ending the hour prematurely by telling the patient that I was ill and needed to end the session. I would sometimes 'pass the time' by counting the beats per minute of my radial pulse. I was initially unaware that there was anything odd about my taking my pulse despite the fact that this is a practice that has never occurred with any other patient ...

During the period of weeks that followed, I gradually became more able to treat the taking of my pulse, as well as the associated feelings and sensations, as 'analytic objects' (Bion, 1962; Green, 1993; Ogden, 1994), i.e. as a reflection of an unconscious construction being generated by the patient and myself, or more accurately being generated by the 'intersubjective analytic third.' I began to be able to link the experience of holding my own wrist (in the act of taking my pulse) with what I now suspected to be a need literally to feel human warmth in an effort to reassure myself that I was alive and healthy. This brought with it a profound shift in my understanding of a great many aspects of my experience with Ms N. I felt moved by the patient's tenacity in telling me seemingly pointless stories for more than 18 months. It occurred to me that these stories had been offered with the unconscious hope that I might find (or create) a point to the stories thereby creating a point (a feeling of coherence, direction, value and authenticity) for the patient's life. I had previously been conscious of my own fantasy of feigning illness in order to escape the stagnant deadness of the sessions, but I had not understood that this 'excuse' reflected an unconscious fantasy that I was being made ill by prolonged exposure to the lifelessness of the analysis.

This example highlights the importance of being able to be curious about and value our own thought process, our function as a container in a non-judgmental way. I believe that this nonjudgmental approach to our own inner thought processes (reverie) is a difficult ideal to achieve, and that we are all susceptible to having our inner sadistic objects criticize our analytic behavior, our not living up to our psychoanalytic ideal.

In relation to the importance of the analyst's capacity to accept him/herself, warts and all, Symington (1983) describes the centrality for Bion of valuing the freedom to think his own thoughts and not feel pressured by external or internal expectations to think in a particular way. Symington illustrates this aspect of the container function in a brief discussion between Bion and an analyst who presented a conundrum in his work with a patient in a supervisory seminar. It is important to note that Bion was not just providing a commentary, a didactic approach emphasizing information or theory, but was also functioning in a procedural way, enacting the importance of being able to think one's own thoughts and resist being pressured by the patient, supervisee, or social norms. I can imagine Bion speaking in a marked way, highlighting the multiple levels of meaning in the concrete, paranoid schizoid communication.

> A. She wants sex with other men besides her husband, therefore in her view she must be a whore. She's afraid that if she got a divorce from her husband she would run around and have sex with all sorts of men – behave like a free whore.
> B. In view of what you are saying I think I would try to draw her attention to the way in which she wishes to limit my freedom about what I call her. It is just as much a limitation if the patient wants you to give the correct interpretation. Why shouldn't I be free to form my own opinion that she's a whore, or that she is something quite different? Why be angry with me because in fact I am free to come to my own conclusions?
> A. Her fear is that your own conclusion will be that she is a whore.
> B. But why shouldn't I be allowed to come to that conclusion?
> A. So you conclude that she is a whore – now where are you?
> B. But I haven't said that I do. The point I want to show is that there is a wish to limit my freedom of thought.
>
> (pp. 15–16)

This brief illustration emphasizes Bion's belief in the importance of not being limited by either the patient's or the analyst's desire, which can be thought of as a precondition of the containing function. We can see that he is trying to refocus this 'what if' paranoid moment into an 'as if' depressive experience. Bion's (1967) assertion of his independence is a version of his often-quoted statement of entering each session without memory or desire, reflecting the importance of the analyst's ability to be free of any limitations that would reflect the paranoid schizoid organization of thought. Symbolization is dependent on the analyst being a secure container open to multiple meanings generated within the analytic situation.

Recent developments in Kleinian theory emphasized the process of dreaming as a further transformation of Bion's container contained model, including reverie, alpha function, and the capacity to transform unconscious experience (beta elements) into meaningful symbolic experiences. This work extends Bion's (1962) concept of waking dream states, that dreaming occurs continuously and is not simply a function of sleep but is an important aspect of how analysts and parents are able to process patients' and children's projective identifications and facilitate growth and the capacity to symbolize experience. Ogden (2004) poetically describes dreaming as the critical process in analysis and, most importantly, as a means of doing the unconscious work of symbolizing unconscious experience.

> A person consults a psychoanalyst because he is in emotional pain, which, unbeknownst to him, he is either unable to dream (i.e., unable to do unconscious psychological work) or is so disturbed by what he is dreaming that his dreaming is disrupted. To the extent that he is unable to dream his emotional experience, the individual is unable to change, or to grow, or to become anything other than who he has been. The patient and analyst engage in an experiment within the terms of the psychoanalytic situation that is designed to generate conditions in which the analysand (with the analyst's participation) may become better able to dream his undreamt and interrupted dreams. The dreams dreamt by the patient and analyst are at the same time their own dreams (and reveries) and those of a third subject who is both and neither patient and analyst.

In a very interesting paper, Ogden (2007) expands the idea of dreaming to a form of analytic discourse in which the quotidian content of the conversation becomes metaphorized so that the elements of the conversation, like the elements of a dream, take on multiple symbolic meanings. Ogden describes this form of conversation as talking like dreaming, in which we may utilize non-linear, dreamlike associations in discussions of books, movies, and historic or current events, which, like poems, create personal meaning, increasing the patient's ability to utilize dreamlike alpha function in apprehending his/her life and to "dream him/her self into existence".

Ferro (2009) utilizes Bion's concept of the waking dream state to describe the analytic process as one in which patients' concrete narratives, organized through an evacuative process and experienced as concrete actual events in the world, become transformed into symbolic, metaphoric, depressive experiences having multiple meanings. One important element in the Kleinian view is that the unconscious is always organizing the subject's experience and perceptions, which, like Klein's initial concept of phantasy, represent early proto-emotions and proto-sensory experiences which exert pressure on the individual and others through processes of splitting and projective identification. Ferro (2006, 2012) argues that the contemporary Kleinian perspective shifts the focus of the psychoanalytic endeavor from an emphasis on content to the development of the unconscious mind (the container) as an instrument for dreaming, feeling, and thinking. Ferro, like Ogden and other contemporary Kleinians, becomes a participant in a process of reverie, of mutual affective elaboration of the events presented in the analytic discourse. Ferro (2009) states:

> In the absence of this capacity to transform protoemotions and protosensoriality into pictograms (of the waking dream state), the analyst will need to cooperate, perhaps even using his own reveries, in the co-construction of the patient's α-sequences, thus enabling the patient to develop an α-function and containing capacity (♀) of his own and eventually allowing its stable introjection.

Ferro (2009) presents an interesting clinical application of this idea, suggesting that we interpret everything a patient says as if it is part of a dream, and that the analyst silently imagine each sentence that the patient says as preceded by the statement "I had a dream ..." It is very interesting that when I have suggested to a supervisee that they do this, the meaning of a patient's dialogue changes, and the analyst is able to feel free to have a more imaginative sense of what the patient is saying. Like other suggestions, this approach of bringing the idea of the waking dream state forward allows us to think of unconscious processes as central to both the patient's intersubjective and intrasubjective experiences.

Notes

1 The controversial discussion between Melanie Klein and Anna Freud created an important split in the development of psychoanalytic theory between those who followed Anna Freud, developing ego psychology, and those following Melanie Klein, emphasizing a focus on unconscious processes.

2 This observation has been found to be somewhat true in recent neuropsychological findings where the earlier-developing amygdala encodes non-verbal memories in the implicit memory system, and the later-developing hippocampus encodes memories in the later-developing explicit memory system.

3 See descriptions of 'mirror neurons' for a possible neuropsychological substrate for this experience.

4 This concept is similar to Fonagy et al.'s concept of psychic equivalence.

5 From a more contemporary perspective, we can think of the container as something like a computer program and the contained as the data that the computer program utilizes in the development of meaning.

Chapter 5

Language, Metaphor and the Unconscious

Introduction

Freud's seminal idea of a hierarchical relationship between the conscious, pre-conscious, and unconscious systems, or the structural model of the superego, ego, and id, functioned as the operational basis for the free association method, which until recently has been the single algorithm of clinical work incapsulated in Freud's (1915a) notion of making the unconscious conscious. Freud's idea of making the unconscious conscious, representing an implicit positivist perspective and privileging rational objective language and experience, became the universal standard for psychoanalytic and non-psychoanalytic therapy. As a surprising example of this universal standard, CBT patients are thought of as suffering from maladaptive thought processes – irrational, unconscious beliefs – which are corrected[1] in CBT therapy by learning a more rational approach to these belief systems.

The term 'conscious thought' – and its derivatives – has two meanings which are often not made explicit. From a technical perspective, consciousness or conscious thought refers to the products of the CNS or aspects of the ego functioning in a rational, adaptive mode; however, consciousness is often used as a synonym for awareness, which is closer to the everyday meaning of consciousness. In classical psychoanalysis, consciousness was thought of as representing 'higher levels' of rational, mature thought, and the unconscious was thought to represent 'lower levels' of immature, irrational, impulse-driven behavior and thought. These aspects of the

DOI: 10.4324/9781003058274-6

concepts of conscious and unconscious thought suggest an implicit set of values defining normality and psychopathology which have remained unquestioned.

This chapter will focus on the influence of two theorists who developed their concepts of conscious and unconscious thought independently from each other; however, each theorist raised similar issues for our understanding of the relationship between conscious and unconscious structures as linguistic experiences. Lacan and Matte Blanco each suggested different views of conscious and unconscious thought, the impact of external reality, and the question of what is normal or mature, which has been deeply embedded in our concepts of consciousness, rational thought and maturity. Matte Blanco and Lacan did not privilege conscious thought over unconscious thought, developing theories in which these were independent, parallel structures in which experience is differentially represented in the external world and the subjective inner world of unconscious thought. Both Lacan and Matte Blanco turned to Freud's (1900) dream theory as the model of the unconscious and how unconscious processes create meaning. In focusing on Freud's conception of the function and organization of dreams, they moved away from drive theory and the sense of the unconscious as representing immature and socially destructive forces and, like the Kleinians, thought of the unconscious as a system of dreamlike processes which create meaning and organize our experience of external reality.

Lacan

In contemporary psychoanalysis, it is important to recognize Lacan's (Dor, 1997) contribution to our understanding of metaphor and language. Unlike most of his contemporary European and American colleagues who conceptualized human experience from a biological perspective, Lacan and analysts associated with the Frankfurt School (Newirth, 2015), thought of psychoanalysis as embedded within social science, anthropology, economic theory, and linguistics. Two major influences on Lacan's (2006) reframing of psychoanalysis, which he described as a "return to Freud,"[2] were Claude Lévi-Strauss, the structural anthropologist, and Roman

Jakobson, the linguist. In reconceptualizing psychoanalysis within the context of culture rather than biology, Lacan notes that, as psychological beings, our lives are an extension of a family system which is contextualized in its history. He uses the idea of the 'Name of the Father' to represent our being embedded in multiple levels of historical organizations of gender, family, tribe, and culture and metaphorically suggest, as part of his linguistic approach, that our lives were 'written' well before we became sentient beings, in the roles and expectations that awaited our arrival. Our lives were written in the conscious and unconscious fantasies and expectations which were part of our legacies at birth. On a clinical level, the Lacanian question, "what do you know about your name," reflects this structural issue and often opens productive paths to be investigated in analysis. Lacan (2006) was particularly critical of, and rejected, ego psychology and its emphasis on adapting to reality. It is interesting and mysterious why Lacan continued to use Freudian language rather than developing an original set of theoretical propositions, as did Sullivan, with whom there are many parallels. I imagine, like Freud, Lacan had a strong missionary zeal and wished to convert the classical psychoanalysts of his time to his new perspective. This effort failed and sadly resulted in his 'excommunication' from the International Psychoanalytic Association.

Lacan (Dor, 1997) redefined the Oedipal situation and the idea of castration as a universal experience in which the child had the inevitable experience of the coming of language, the imposition of culture on the child's imaginary experience of being the thing that makes mother complete and filled with joy. Lacan, in his humorous way, defined this experience as the No/Name of the Father, because these words in French (*non, nom*) sound the same and can only be differentiated by viewing the context. More important than the sound of the French words, the No/Name of the Father is not simply a personal experience, but a universal experience of having to give up the infantile experience, or fantasy,[3] that one is the source of one's mother's joy, a very romantic view which leaves us in a permanent existential state of longing for a lost paradise, a state in which disappointment is inevitable. Lacan's (2006) first paper, "The Mirror Stage," described the register of the imaginary in which the child feels/believes that he/she represents everything that mother desires. The imaginary is one of three registers of experience, along with the symbolic and the real, which Lacan believes structure the individual's experience and function in various interactive and complex, intersubjective ways.

He believed that the inevitable coming of language, the No/Name of the Father, initiates the register of the symbolic and disrupts the child's purely affective and immediate relationship with the mother, recognizing that she has other desires, which initiates a dawning awareness that there are rules, existential truths, and cultural consequences that each person must learn. Psychopathology for Lacan involves different strategies for attempting to avoid the inevitable necessity of accepting castration, the No/Name of the Father and the symbolic register. This "wall of language" (Dor, 1997), the symbolic, separates the child's intense desires and beliefs in his/her specialness from the culture's requirement that the child follow rules (the law/lore), which simultaneously splits the mind into two parallel structures, an unconscious center of desire and subjectivity and a conscious center of who we are supposed to be, the self as an ego-ideal, describing the duality of who we should be to get the other's approval, as opposed to who we discover we are and what we really desire.

Lacan believed that these now split-off – or repressed – desires can only be represented linguistically through structures of metaphor and metonymy, which he derived from Freud's concept of dreams. Both Lacan and Matte Blanco thought that dream work, processes of condensation and displacement, and metaphoric and metonymic structures, represent the structure of unconscious thought. It is the advent of language, of the law and the No/Name of the Father, which creates the split in the subject between desire and the wish to receive the other's approval, the imaginary. Lacan (Dor, 1997) playfully illustrates his idea of metaphor as expressing unconscious and unspoken desires and beliefs, citing Freud's famous comment on arriving in America for the Clark University lectures: "I am bringing the plague to America"! Freud's use of the metaphor of "the plague" probably represented his belief that the culture of America would find the psychoanalytic emphasis on self-reflection, destructiveness, and sexuality anathema. I believe that Freud's use of the metaphor of the plague also represented his wish to infect us with the disease of psychoanalysis that he suffered from.

Lacan's concept of the imaginary is linked with the mirror stage and emphasizes the belief that appearance will lead to happiness, that the image, either actual or linguistic, is the thing that will lead to happiness, but inevitably fails and results in a lack of satisfaction and hunger for the next thing (metonymy) which we believe will lead to happiness. I always think of myself trying on a new suit and how well I think I look in the store's mirror, as I stand extra tall and pull in my stomach; of course, when I get home, I find that the new suit does not make me into the person I wished I was and I experience the inevitable lack and disappointment that this new suit will not make me inordinately lovable.

The imaginary is insatiable, always demanding the next experience of becoming the thing that everyone wants, a return to the infantile state of merger with mother. For Lacan, these imaginary experiences are represented by empty words in the analytic relationship, language without self-reflection. For Lacan, language, the symbolic, splits the subject and creates the possibility that language may articulate desire and allow the subject to locate him/herself in a system where there is a possibility for self-understanding and acceptance. This understanding is based on a particular form of language involving the capacity to develop metaphors which express the underlying desire and the possibility of self-acceptance. For Lacan, the goal of the analysis is for the subject to speak, to know his/her desire and acknowledge their lack. Lacan describes the end of analysis as the subject's becoming able to "traverse the fantasy," which involves self-acceptance and a recognition that he/she has created, is the author of, his/her life, which was an inevitable outcome of the personal, familial, and cultural forces that he/she was thrown into. Rather than Oedipus Rex, Lacan's theory seems to echo Oedipus at Colonus, where Oedipus, now elderly and blind, comes to recognize that he is not the guilty son who killed his father and married his mother, but was actually part of a movement in history written and spoken by the Delphic Oracle, which allows him to finally accept and understand himself.

Matte Blanco

Matte Blanco (1988) was a Chilean analyst who studied with Klein and, like Lacan, emphasized different forms of language as central to the structure of the unconscious. He conceptualized the mind differently from the traditional hierarchical structural model organized around energy dynamics and anatomy. Rather than using anatomy or energy dynamics as a model for the mind, Matte Blanco focused on the function of conscious and unconscious mentation, developing a dual theory of mental representation, bi-logic, in which conscious and unconscious thought reflected different functions: conscious thought functioned as a means to know and create the external world of things and objects, and unconscious thought functioned to know and create the internal world of affects and subjective meaning. Matte Blanco suggested that consciousness, knowing the external world of objects, utilized asymmetrical logic which differentiated experience in terms of person, place, time, and causality, while unconscious experience was organized and generated by symmetrical logic, which identified and created similarities, dedifferentiating experience in terms of person, place, time, and causality, as in dreams which collapse these dimensions into a surrealist world of images in which one image may represent a series of experiences, linked and identified with each other. Conceptualizing these two modes of processing experience separately allows us to understand many patients who function quite well in the external world, utilizing the asymmetrical mode of thought, but are barely able to function in the emotional world of close and intimate relationships which involves using the symmetrical mode in which these relationships need to be imagined and developed.

Langer (1942), a philosopher and linguist, suggested two similar modes of symbolizing, knowing, and articulating experience, which she described as discursive and presentational symbols. Discursive symbols translate experience from one mode to another, as when we explain experience in terms of history or biology or turn to universal principles and precedents, such as the Oedipus complex, to understand a patient's difficulty with authority. Presentational symbols do not try to explain events but rather attempt to re-create the affective experience of an event, through identification, creating dramatic or artistic experiences. For example, Hamlet brings us into a different state of emotional understanding of struggles with authority than does a discursive explanation of Oedipal or political dynamics. Discursive symbols, like asymmetrical logic, differentiate experience in terms of time, person, place, and causality, while presentational symbols, like symmetrical logic, collapse differences within these dimensions and create an emotional experience, allowing us to become deeply involved in the experience. Picasso's painting of Guernica uses a symmetrical, presentational, dreamlike surrealist mode to represent and evoke an experience of war, death, and destruction, whereas a newspaper article or history of the Spanish Civil War presents the same experience from an asymmetrical, discursive perspective. Again, both represent truth: the former, the emotional, subjective truth, and the latter, the historical, causal, historical truth of war.

Symmetry and asymmetry are alternative, parallel modes of creating meaning and structuring interpretations in psychoanalysis and psychotherapy. Depending on which form of logic we use, the same experience will have different meanings and be understood differently. For example, Matte Blanco (1988) suggests that, when unbearable internal experiences are externalized through pathological projective identification and are not contained or elaborated by another person (parent or therapist), they become experienced asymmetrically as external events: concrete, immutable facts in the external world which cannot be altered. These externalized bits of reality, beta elements, if contained and elaborated by an other, can be thought of as Bion's concept of alpha function, reverie, and dream work, which can be understood as symmetrical processes of affective and symbolic elaboration in which the therapist's identifications and experiences of similarities are a first step in containing and elaborating a patient's dissociated, unconscious, concrete experience.

We can think of the container contained function as a critical part of the interpretive process in which a therapist can use either an asymmetrical strategy, attempting to differentiate time, person, place, and causality, or a symmetrical strategy, in which these differences are collapsed, creating poetic-like experiences of similarities and metaphors which provide an intense affective, presentational experience. For example, a therapist who believes that he/she is being experienced as a mother in the transference may say, using an asymmetrical strategy, "I am not your mother," attempting to help separate the patient from the repetition of past expectations and failed behaviors. Alternatively, using a symmetrical strategy, the therapist may say, "I am your mother," highlighting the current emotional reality of the transference–countertransference experience. Both statements are true; however, they each result in different affective and cognitive experiences for the patient and therapist. The asymmetrical strategy encourages a differentiation of the therapist from the historical object, while the symmetrical strategy encourages the articulation of the affective experience of being a child in a nurturing relationship.

In describing the mind as a bi-logical structure, Matte Blanco presented two alternative models, two ways of conceptualizing the relationship between conscious and unconscious mentation, or asymmetrical and symmetrical processes. The first model (Matte Blanco, 1975) involved a hierarchical view of the relationship between asymmetry and symmetry, with asymmetry (rational thought) at the top of the hierarchy and symmetry at the bottom of a set of potential experiences of the two modes being combined in various proportions. This hierarchical view would seem to conform to Freud's idea of secondary process thought superseding primary process thought and support the idea that the analyst's goal would be to translate patients' symmetrical experiences into more rational and adaptable organizations. The second model of the relationship between asymmetry and symmetry that Matte Blanco (1988) suggests is contained in his statement of the absolute antinomy between symmetry and asymmetry. I interpret this second model as suggesting that these are two independent and parallel forms of thought which can each represent the same experience using a different form of logic, as in the above example of Guernica, where we can understand how both symmetrical presentational symbols and asymmetrical, historic explanations express the truth of war. Matte Blanco (1988) also suggests that there are some emotional experiences, such as love, that cannot adequately be represented in the asymmetrical mode and can only be represented and expressed in the symmetrical mode. For example, one would not be very welcome telling one's lover that he/she compares fairly well with other possible lovers as opposed to saying that he/she is the one and only person in the world, and that the sun rises and sets with his/her smile. Obviously, both are true; love is both transient and infinite; however, most emotional and intimate experiences are best represented with symmetrical language, and, as in this example, the symmetrical mode develops metaphors which collapse differences and creates strong, affective experiences and identifications.

Mancia (2006) integrates Matte Blanco's ideas within the context of neuropsychology and presents an interesting argument that the unrepressed unconscious – schemas of intense early affective experiences which have been mediated by the amygdala and stored in implicit memory – can be thought of as part of the symmetrical unconscious described by Matte Blanco. He presents a great deal of recent neuropsychological findings contrasting implicit memory and non-verbal emotional schemas – involving the use of procedural learning and symmetrical processes (B.P.C.S.G. et al., 1998) which underlie implicit relational schemas, dreams, transference, trust, and other intimate experiences – with those of explicit declarative memory in which verbal, autobiographical memories are used to describe external reality and history. These two organizations of memory, the implicit and the explicit, have been thought of as the non-repressed and the repressed structures of the unconscious, with the former utilizing symmetrical logic and the latter utilizing asymmetrical logic.

In order to address questions raised by the parallel functions of symmetry and asymmetry as alternative ways of organizing, apprehending, and generating experience, I developed a two-dimensional psychoanalytic model of thinking (Newirth, 2003) combining concepts of the paranoid schizoid and depressive modes of thought with the dimensions of asymmetry and symmetry. This develops a two-by-two model integrating the Kleinian dialectic of the paranoid schizoid and the depressive positions, in which there is a movement from concrete to symbolic thought, and Matte Blanco's concepts of symmetry and asymmetry to represent the different modes of thought used in the external world and the internal world. In this model, the concrete thought of the paranoid schizoid position occurs in both symmetrical and asymmetrical modes, contrasting the intense affective experiences of persecutory anxiety, terror, and nightmares with the frustrating experiences of obsessional states, literal responses, and the slicing of reality into smaller and smaller segments. The symbolic experiences within both the paranoid schizoid and depressive positions involve transcendent states of love, merger, and poetic language with asymmetrical experiences in the depressive position of abstract thought, historic and genetic explanations, and the law which regulates our behavior in the external world. The different experiences described in the schematic diagram in Figure 5.1 are meant as illustrations of the interaction of the Kleinian dialectic of the paranoid schizoid and depressive positions and Matte Blanco's description of the antinomy of the symmetrical and asymmetrical organizations of thought through which we can compare representations developed in the inner world with those developed in the external world.

Independent of the matrix in Figure 5.1, Ferro (2009, p. 201) also integrates Matte Blanco's theory with Kleinian thought and suggests that out of the "symmetrical proto-mind an infinity of derivatives represented in words can emerge, but they will never resume or capture it totally. Words are nets that surround emotion

	Symmetry		Asymmetry	
The paranoid schizoid position: **concrete thought processes**	1.	Body symptoms	1.	Obsessional states
	2.	Nightmares	2.	Collection of details
	3.	Persecutory anxiety	3.	Literal responses
	4.	States of terror	4.	Fragmentation anxiety
	5.	Falling through space	5.	Splitting or slicing reality
The depressive position: **symbolic** **thought processes**	1.	Dreams and creative fantasies	1.	Abstract thought
	2.	Empathy	2.	Inferential process
	3.	Poetry	3.	Discursive symbols
	4.	Dedifferentiation of self and other	4.	Genetic, transference interpretations
	5.	Transcendence and ecstatic experience	5.	The law
	6.	Synchronic time	6.	Diachronic time

Figure 5.1 The Matrix of Mental Experience.

and circumscribe it but they do not replace it." Symmetrical formulations, like reverie, create metaphoric or poetic language that expresses and generates graspable meanings for unconscious content. Many theorists have focused on the concept of metaphor as a symmetrical form of unconscious representation in this expanding transformational model of the mind. Metaphor has the psychological qualities of symmetrical, symbolic organizations of experience, like dream thoughts, humor (Newirth, 2018), and presentational symbols. Metaphor has been a central concern for psychoanalysis for many decades. Metaphors have been used to connect theory and technique, as in Theodore Reik's (1959) idea of "listening with the third ear," which expresses something more experiential and emotional than Freud's pragmatic concept of "free-floating attention" and Civitarese's and Ferro's (2013) concept of the analytic relationship as a field, like an electromagnetic field, in which there are continuous effects of the different psychological particles. Clinicians have traditionally used metaphors as an interpretive device in clinical practice, and more recently theorists have begun to think of metaphor as more than a linguistic trope, as an element of mental structure which creates meaning in the intersubjective realm of emotional and intimate relationships.

Fonagy and Target (2007) discuss the contemporary development of concepts of metaphor as an aspect of our human potential for making meaning, differentiating current concepts of embodied cognition (Weinberger & Stoycheva, 2021) from earlier concepts which treated the mind as separated from bodily experience. Particularly important in their assessment of these developments is the work of contemporary linguists Lakoff and Johnson (1999) and the French linguist Fonagy (as cited in Fonagy, 2008). These contemporary linguists believe that metaphors are not simple linguistic constructions but emerge from and express bodily experiences, as when we feel the actual pain of a broken heart or feel uplifted by a lover's smile. Embodied metaphors develop in both intrasubjective and intersubjective relationships, often beginning as sensory experiences, gestures, and enactments which express moments of intersubjective conjunction and disjunction. Although Fonagy and Target do not point this out, we may understand these metaphors developing as concrete experiences, gestures, and signs, which are potentially empathic and communicative, perhaps developing an experience of identification through the mirror neuron system (Ginot, 2009; Wolf et al., 2001) and slowly become patterned as RIGS, "representations of interactions that have been generalized" (Stern, 1985), and then being expressed through symbolic, metaphorical statements. Schore's (2011) suggestion of direct affective communication between the right brain and right brain of individuals in an intimate relationship, and the operation of mirror neurons as the neurological substrate for emphatic and intimate relatedness reflect presentational and procedural aspects of learning which develop in the intimate relationship between parent and child and patient and therapist.

The theory of embodied cognition suggests that metaphors and gestures develop simultaneously as representations, body experience, gestures, actions, and metaphoric enactments, which bring a continuous sense of affective bodily experience to intersubjective relationships. Fonagy and Target (2007) state that:

> all mental acts are metaphorical and through metaphor have physical as well as abstract (symbolic) meanings. The action of the thought carries metaphoric unconscious meaning. When we "grasp an idea" we may experience a feeling of well-being or "goodness" because unconsciously we reunite with the primary object. When we "grope for a meaning" at the level of gesture we find empty space where a warm body should be, and the affect state generated is one of vacuum or emptiness. When we "seize on an idea" we in a real sense jump on top of it and thus feel excited and triumphant, like a toddler claiming omnipotent control.

(p. 438)

Fonagy and Target link the development of the capacity to use metaphors and metaphoric enactments with attachment relationships, suggesting that patients who have had difficulty in early attachment relationships will also have difficulty in developing the capacity for verbal and enacted processes of metaphoric expression. The concept of metaphors and metaphoric enactments expands our discussion of the concept of symmetrical presentational symbols in the clinical situation and the development of the capacity to transform experience from concrete signs to symbolic meaning.

Contemporary Kleinian (Civitarese & Ferro, 2013; Ferro, 2009; Ogden, 2007, 2010) analysts have begun to approach their clinical work as a process of developing metaphors in their relationship with patients. This focus on metaphors is a clinical or pragmatic development of the theoretical, abstract concepts of symbolization, alpha function, and the container contained model of the analytic relationship. Ferro's description of the importance of metaphors in the analytic dialogue echoes his (2009, p. 206) comments about embodied metaphors that link these unconscious processes to bodily experience:

> They are sensible ideas ... that is to say, they combine emotion and thought. They therefore restore a bodily element to the mind; they reunite psyche and soma; they reforge the "psychosomatic collusion" (Winnicott, 1974, p. 104) that is the foundation of subjectivity; they are dreams that create reality and give it a personal meaning.

Ogden (2010) emphasizes the process of metaphorization as an outcome of the container contained process, including the sequence of collapse, reverie, and symbolization. It is important in understanding this clinical process to recognize that the analytic dialogue emphasizes the development of metaphors and embodied metaphorical experiences which allow for the transformation of concrete signs in the development of subjective meaning. Ogden (2010) differentiates three forms of thinking: magical thinking, dream thinking, and transformational thinking. Magical thinking reflects thinking within the paranoid schizoid position where what is real is what is in my mind, a version of symbolic or psychic equivalence, and we might also think of this as an aspect of the Lacanian imaginary. For example, denial would involve the individual not wanting to know something and erasing it from consciousness. Dream thinking involves our capacity to create meaning using reverie, symmetrical symbolic thinking, metaphoric enactments, and presentational symbols. Transformational thinking is a rare event in which a metaphor or metaphoric enactment alters the fundamental organization of meaning for an individual, as when one shifts from a habitual understanding of self and other, of relational structures, to a new, more fluid understanding in which old categories become replaced by new perceptions and symbolic expressions. Ogden (2010) uses the example of Christ's switching from the rule of law to a sense of personal relatedness and responsibility when he said, to a crowd that would stone a woman for committing adultery:

> When Jesus stands, he does not reply to the question that has been posed. He says something utterly unexpected and does so in the simplest of words – a sentence in which all but two of the fifteen words are monosyllabic: "He that is without sin among you, let him first cast a stone at her." Jesus does not address the question of whether to obey the law or break the law, and instead poses a completely different, highly enigmatic question: how does one bring to bear one's own experience of being human, which includes one's own sinful acts, to the problem of responding to the behavior of another person? And further, the passage raises the question of whether any person has the right to stand in judgment of another person. At the end of the passage, Jesus renounces any intention of standing in judgment of the woman: "Neither do I condemn thee."
>
> (p. 334)

Ogden's concept of transformational thinking involves symmetry, presentational symbols, and is a form of metaphoric enactment. This illustration of transformational thinking is a form of altering a fixed set of unconscious expectations, a movement from the external rules of behavior to a highly personal, subjective moment – what Lacan might have thought about as traversing the fantasy in a highly symbolic way.

Notes

1   Unlike the collaborative approaches developed by psychoanalysis, CBT and other behavioral treatments have maintained an authoritarian approach in which the therapist is largely in charge.

2 This is a very complex statement which is often quoted but rarely, if ever explained and, like much of Lacan's work, has multiple meanings.
3 Think of the story of Adam and Eve in the Garden of Eden as the end of the child's experience of paradise.

Chapter 6

The Unconscious and the Contemporary Subject

Introduction

The contemporary subject and the structure and experience of the unconscious are quite different from the unconscious that Freud wrote about in the late nineteenth and early twentieth century. Freud's early work with patients focused on three dimensions of the unconscious: the unconscious as the structure that determines psychopathology and health, unconscious processes of repression as the focus of psychoanalytic treatment, and the alternative forms of representation in conscious as contrasted with unconscious forms of representation, as a dreamlike process in which meaning is both created and often repeated over and over again in nightmare-like experiences. The contemporary theories which were presented in this book approached these three dimensions from different perspectives, some of which overlap, and some focus on different dynamic processes. Almost all contemporary theories have a two-person perspective focusing on both family experience in the early environment as a critical factor in the development and organization of the unconscious and the transference–countertransference relationship as a complex two-person situation. Most psychoanalytic theories involve a pragmatic approach in which explicit verbal interpretations and implicit enactments bring the patient's unconscious into the dynamic playground of the psychoanalytic relationship. Finally, these contemporary theories differ in their emphasis on phenomenological approaches to the unconscious, which remain closer to Freud's topographic model,

DOI: 10.4324/9781003058274-7

and those that have developed a structural view of the unconscious, again like Freud's less experience-near model of the ego, id, and superego.

I want to return to the Introduction where I used three movies to present the evolving historic view of the unconscious: first as the feared monster within; second as the confusion between our view of ourself as a bad, destructive person or a good but guilty person; and finally as the experience of the unconscious as a sense of deadness, meaninglessness, undifferentiated from all others and propelled towards constant action, often without satisfaction or joy. T.S. Elliot's prescient 1925 poem "The Hollow Men" anticipated the contemporary subject's emptiness and inability to create a meaningful life or, in Ogden's (2004) unique phrase, to dream oneself into existence.

The movie *World War Z* used the world of zombies to represent the insatiable hunger and the profound sense of deadness, the inability to create meaning in one's life as the core of the contemporary subject and his stunted unconscious. I would like to describe my work[1] with a patient who I see as an archetype of the contemporary patient. This patient began therapy because he experienced severe depression and appeared to be in a hopeless state of despair. As often happens in work with these patients, I was deeply affected by his sense of deadness and felt overwhelmed with doubt about myself as an analyst and the entire analytic enterprise. After a long period of being unable to think, of experiencing myself as a broken container (Newirth, 2018), I became able to begin a process of talking like dreaming (Ogden, 2007) with this patient, who seems to have not developed the capacity to dream, to transform beta elements into alpha experiences, and was stuck in the external world of facts. He experienced himself as filled with guilt, going through the motions of living without any sense of being genuinely alive. In the following case illustration, I focus on a series of transformational moments, what the B.P.C.S.G. et al. (1998) would call "now moments," moments in which there is a potential for change, for movement from the concreteness of the paranoid schizoid position to the development of the capacity for waking dream experience within the analytic relationship. In focusing on these transformative moments, we can track the development of the capacity for reverie, dream thoughts, and the generative unconscious.

Clinical Illustration

I have been working with Mr. X for almost two years. It is interesting to me that I am calling him Mr. X, when, in the past, I have always assigned first names to patients that I write about. I think this choice of name reflects my experience of his overwhelming sense of himself as an object, lifeless, simply an impersonal example of what it means to be a human being, no different from the millions of other people populating the earth. Mr. X began to see me several years after he had broken off his engagement to a woman who seemed to have been the driving force in their relationship. He continued to feel depressed and, although not actively suicidal, expressed his feeling that there was no reason to go on living. He described the end of that relationship as having evolved over several months, during which time he struggled with the idea that he was "supposed to propose to her and become engaged." During this time of inner struggle, his perception of his fiancée changed: he began to ruminate about her appearance, her physical features, thinking that she had become extremely unattractive, and, as a result of these thoughts which fragmented her body, he stopped feeling attracted to her, becoming critical, distant, and hopeless about being with her. I believe that this reflected his moving into a largely paranoid schizoid state in which he both felt persecuted by his thoughts and began to experience the world as a collection of broken, concrete, part objects. His thought process became dominated by rumination, highly abstract, asymmetrical thoughts about his future. He would project his life into an infinite experience of space and time, seeing both himself and his fiancée getting progressively older, moving to the suburbs, having children, retiring, becoming ill, going through all of the motions of life until death finally claimed them. In short, for him, it all felt pointless and hopeless. This deadened and deadening experience of going through the motions of living was a constant and repetitive way that he spoke of his experiences at work and in his very limited social life. His experience of desire and ambition had become seriously impaired; he talked about his lack of "libido" and lack of interest in women. As pointed out by Grotstein (1995), he had foreclosed all ideas of pleasure and the possibilities of play through which he could create a life of his own. He had diagnosed himself as "depressed" and had seen a psychiatrist who prescribed anti-depressant medication, which did not help, and who attempted to motivate him to see the more positive aspects of his life. These efforts did not bear fruit.

Mr. X was a successful software engineer who seemed to work very hard at his job. I thought that Mr. X presented the paradox of many contemporary patients. He was able to successfully navigate the external world of things and abstract, asymmetrical thought, while having no pleasure from his apparent success in the world. He seemed to largely operate in the mode of psychic or symbolic equivalence, living in a concrete paranoid world in which he was controlled by external events and the impersonal forces of fate and time; he was simply an object without any sense of subjectivity or agency.

Mr. X did not seem to have a capacity to utilize the pretend mode, to use imagination or metaphors to generate new possibilities in his life; all was fixed; he lived and spoke in a passive voice, feeling defeated by the inevitable disappointments that occurred when he would momentarily attempt to step out of his very limited world. Although I do not believe that I shared my association with him, I felt that his view of himself, me, and other people was much like we were ants living in an ant colony, where we had to follow an impersonal plan, like leaf-cutter ants unrelentingly marching in single file, carrying leaves on their backs into the anthill, where the leaves are turned into food for the colony.

During the early period of our work, Mr. X always appeared depressed and lethargic, head hung over, speaking in a slow monotone voice, presenting his experience as if speaking from a faraway point in outer space. Our sessions often seemed fragmented, dead and deadening. The sessions were filled with detailed accounts of events in the external world with little thought or self-reflection. As an analyst, I often felt embarrassed, unable to think, filled with guilt and questioning my competence, while being distracted by seemingly irrelevant thoughts and watching the time pass. In retrospect, I wonder how much of my experiences were a function of projective and introjective identification in which I experienced my thoughts as concrete facts, questioning my value, in a state of psychic or symbolic equivalents. I think of these sessions with Mr. X as being bombarded by beta elements, concrete, disconnected moments of his life, presented as absolute facts, which I could not make sense of or interpret. My ability to think and generate images felt completely absent. I felt thrown into the chaos of the unsymbolized chaotic universe, knocked down by wave after wave of transference–countertransference failure.

I often found myself questioning what I was doing and why Mr. X continued. At these moments, I find Bion's idea of –K, which describes experiences of being unable to think, as providing the emotional support necessary to tolerate such periods of chaos and to feel safe, knowing that eventually the emerging threads of reverie will initiate the development of proto-symbols, 'pictograms,' which could potentially develop into more meaningful experiences of the emerging, unformulated unconscious fantasies that are being evacuated into the analytic field.

Mr. X arrived for a session in what seemed like a severe state of dissociation; he was very depressed, seemed faraway, head hung over, speaking in his soft monotone. He began talking about an ongoing problem at work and his not knowing if he would continue to be employed. This was a frequent theme, which he presented each time as if it were a new experience and an absolute fact. He continued, saying that he was not sure if he wanted to be employed and began questioning the point of his work and working at all! He said that he was hardly eating and continued to question the point of living. He described his daily cycle of getting up, eating, exercising, going to work, coming home, eating, and going to bed, only to repeat this sequence over and over again. I knew that his apartment was totally barren, without any possibility of entertainment or distraction. As Mr. X continued to raise the rhetorical question of why he should continue to live, I was aware of the power of his suicidal preoccupation and was afraid of directly interrogating this question. I was afraid that any explicit discussion of suicide would provide support for his argument of the pointlessness of life. At this moment, I could not think of many reasons to go on living – I am not sure if this reflected a part of me, or if it represented a complete collapse of the containing function, a concrete symmetrization in which my experience of the analytic dyad became completely merged as a symbiotic object.[2] I felt concerned, frightened, and rather impotent as an analyst. As I sat with these feelings, an image (pictogram) began to form in my mind. It was like a scene in an old movie, a somewhat disheveled prisoner, in a depressing, empty prison cell, was crossing off the days of the weeks, months, and years, marking off the days of his life, until the end. It was an image of a man unable to alter his fate, only able to count the days till the end of his sentence. It was a very clear and persistent image which I decided to describe to Mr. X and tell him the reverie that our conversation had stimulated in me. As I write, I am aware that I did not know if this image was a reflection of me or of Mr. X. Which one of us was the prisoner counting the days of his life? As in a dream, there is a great deal of fluidity between the characters of my reverie as we switch positions; again, we might question whether this was his dream or mine.

To my surprise, Mr. X responded with more enthusiasm than I had previously seen. In a lively voice, he said my image reminded him of the old television series *Gunsmoke* that he had watched all the time as a boy. He had spent many hours alone in his room, watching and rewatching episodes of *Gunsmoke* and other Westerns. He told me that he had never talked about having been so completely involved in watching Westerns on TV, that they had influenced him a great deal, and he had both consciously and unconsciously adopted the role of the isolated hero of the Westerns. The session became taken up with the themes and characters from *Gunsmoke*, as we each brought forward favorite characters from the show. He identified with the marshal, Matt Dillon, and we talked about how, in this show and other Westerns, the hero never gets the girl but always leaves town having simply "gotten rid of the bad guys." We continued to talk in this excited way, sharing our associations, our reverie, talking about old Westerns that seemed to function metaphorically as a waking dream that we were mutually creating. As the session ended, I remembered the last scene in the movie *Shane*, in which the main character, after having saved the homesteaders from the bad guys, rides out of town leaving a potential family behind, while a little boy named Joey is calling "Shane, Shane come back, come back, Shane." Again, in retrospect, I think that I was that little boy calling Mr. X, implying that we could play together and perhaps develop a different, less lonely unconscious script.

This session highlighted the difference between a child who plays alone, as Mr. X did, watching Westerns alone in his room, which Fonagy and Target (2007) describe as a dissociative process, and a child who plays with others, which leads to the development of the capacity for symbolization, or mentalization, being with others in a symbolic, pretend mode, through which people mutually create meaning and their subjective worlds.

In the following session, Mr. X began talking about our mutual reverie about Westerns. He said that, when he thought about it, he felt that one of the lessons he took from watching those Westerns was, "I would rather be right than succeed." This statement captured a central value of Mr. X, one that kept him from pursuing more pleasurable experiences. I reflected on his wearing a 'white hat' and said that I actually preferred wearing a 'black hat' and how easy it was in the Westerns to know what was right and what was wrong, who was good and who was bad. Although our relationship was becoming more playful and Mr. X was becoming more able to reflect on our process and on aspects of his life, the overwhelming sense of futility seemed to continue to organize his experience and our sessions. He was committed to being the lonely hero, doing good and being right and continuing to live without pleasure or satisfaction. The goal of facilitating Mr. X's ability to use more imaginative and metaphoric processes in developing both intimate relationships and in understanding his own life experiences was still a long way off.

A few months later, Mr. X was speaking about the pointlessness of life, seeming resentful of my somewhat optimistic stance, as our relationship became warmer as a result of the shared experience of being in the dream world of the Westerns. In response to Mr. X's descriptions of the futility of his life, I began to feel trapped and thought about the Prisoner's Dilemma game that I had used in my dissertation. Because of his background in mathematics, I assumed that Mr. X was familiar with the Prisoner's Dilemma game, which he affirmed. This is a game in which there is a choice between a zero-sum and a non-zero-sum outcome, in human terms, to see if you can trust the other player not to betray you. If you cannot trust the other player, it is to your advantage to betray the other player before they betray you and you risk losing maximum money or points. The possible outcomes of the game are that both people trust each other and both can win, both people distrust each other and both lose, or one trusts the other, who betrays the trusting player. The one who betrays gets a big payoff, and the one who trusts gets a big loss. This is an interesting paradigm that has been used to study the dynamics of trust and betrayal, or competition and cooperation, in intersubjective relationships and in organizations. Having introduced this game into our session, I told Mr. X that, when computers play this game, they become stuck in the position of mutual distrust and mutual loss, because the rational solution is not to trust the other who can potentially screw you – the rational solution is not to trust, not to hope for something better. When people play the game, they introduce a possibility of hope, of mutual trust, of success, of mutual pleasure, because they take the chance of trusting the other. I commented that he seems to play the game in an entirely rational way, always accepting a moderate loss over the possibility of winning. We talked about the different strategies of the Prisoner's Dilemma game, and he seemed to be convinced that the only way to play was not to take the chance of winning and to continue in his isolated and hopeless strategy. I felt disheartened at the end of this session, as if I had reinforced his belief system that it is foolish to hope because inevitably you will lose.

Mr. X began the following session seeming more energized than usual and told me that he had seen a trainer and was beginning an exercise program. He said that he asked the trainer, a woman, whether, if he began weight training, that would increase his libido. She reassured him that it would increase his libido and his desire. I felt that this change seemed to reflect a shift in his capacity to imagine himself to be different, to see the possibility of hope, of sexuality and pleasure in the future and in our sessions.

He was beginning to be able to imagine himself, in Ogden's words, to dream himself into existence, and to metaphorize his body as a possible source of strength and sensual pleasure.

These metaphoric moments, including my discussion of the Prisoner's Dilemma game, seemed to facilitate Mr. X's beginning to develop the capacity to transform his archaic, concrete experiences of an unalterable reality (beta fragments) into dreamlike images, imaginative, symbolic experiences, the capacity to use imaginative thought processes in creating a possible future involving subjectivity, desire, and pleasure.

In a session during this phase of our work in which Mr. X was shifting his way of thinking/being to include symbolic, symmetrical, metaphoric processes of the waking dream state, he said that he had been listening to a favorite old song that resulted in his uncontrollable crying. The song was "My Heroes Have Always Been Cowboys," which was originally recorded by Waylon Jennings. When patients mention songs as meaningful associations, I think of these songs as waking dreams that represent unconscious structures or phantasies that generate meaning. I always ask my patients to speak/sing as much of the song as they can. Mr. X spoke some of the lyrics, which I also found to be very moving. The song presents the lonely life of a cowboy who is disconnected from others and is a sad drifter, moving between brief moments of contact with women but unable to maintain any relationship. This moment seemed to illustrate Mr. X's transformation from his lonely, dissociated state of watching Westerns, in a daydream-like (Winnicott, 1971) activity, to an emotional, meaningful, and shared fantasy that we could share and each feel.

I had not seen Mr. X so present in his life as he was when he spoke the lyrics to this song. He said that, after he listened to the song and cried a great deal, he called his mom, and they spoke for a long time in what seemed like a comforting conversation. He also called his ex-fiancée, and they had dinner. He seemed to be reaching out to the women in his life, something that he had not done before. We continued to talk about country-and-western songs that he loved, and the session ended with my talking about the Kris Kristofferson song "Me and Bobby McGee," which describes a contemporary version of a cowboy remembering a lost love and, ironically, ends with powerful, emotional lyrics reflecting Mr. X's cowboy ethic and reprising the loneliness of the song "My Heroes Have Always Been Cowboys." These lyrics symbolize and transform the pain of loss and desire while simultaneously introducing the possibility of hope, as Mr. X moves into a more symbolic, symmetrical state of being.

Mr. X began the next session talking about a weird experience over the weekend when he visited a friend who is extremely successful, married, and has three kids. He felt like he had nothing, was empty, and was nothing, which represented a new experience, one in which he was able to reflect on his life rather than simply feeling like a victim of his fate. This led to his talking about suicide. After talking about suicidal thoughts, which seemed very frightening, he said he would not kill himself because he had promised his mother that he would not kill himself. He began talking about his uncle, who had killed himself and whom he admired and spent a lot of time with when he was a child. In talking about this loss and his continuing confusion about why his uncle had committed suicide, he seemed filled with a new emotional experience of sadness that, paradoxically, felt very alive and emotionally connected.

As this session came to an end, I felt deeply moved and was sorry that we had to end. I said, "I am sorry we have to end," and he said, in a deadened and supposedly reassuring voice, "It's OK, that's the way it is." I thought he rejected my attempt at closeness and said, in an ironic and exaggerated voice, that I know it is OK – that I was simply expressing my feelings, that sometimes I can't stop myself from expressing my feelings. I then, in an ironic voice, differentiated the feeling, human part of me from the business, analyst part of me. I assured him that, from then on, I would try to keep my feelings under control. During this whole enactment, we were both laughing and enjoying my stand-up routine. Again, in retrospect, I wondered about my response and how much of it was a symmetrization of his unspoken loss, of his dissociated feelings, and of complex processes of projective and introjective identification, of the function of the container and contained.

Over the next several months, our sessions had a different tone: we were speaking more to each other and moving back and forth between discussions of the asymmetrical external world and of his more subjective, hopeful, and metaphorical conversations. With this transformation, it has become hard for me to see Mr. X as a zombie-like presence. It is interesting that one of the next themes that emerged involved experiences around his body and some pain that has developed as a result of his earlier intense, ascetic pursuit of yoga. He continued to focus on weight training, becoming stronger and changing his diet from one that was depriving to one that included more variety, and finding eating as a source of pleasure and energy. I understood these evolving conversations about his body from Winnicott's (1975) perspective of his developing greater psychosomatic unity, as well as becoming more integrated rather than experiencing himself as a collection of parts. During this period, in which he was able to be more reflective and also saw the analysis as a collaborative process, he began one session stating that he was feeling bored and empty. I commented that I thought that this was good, because it reflected his ability to imagine that things can be different and more hopeful. He responded to my comment by talking about being more excited at work and about a new project that he was working on.

I want to end by presenting some of Mr. X's comments in a recent session that reflect a change in, and expand, his identification with the cowboy myth and ethic. Mr. X had a long-standing concern that he had ruined his ex-fiancée's life by not marrying her. This was an idea that literally haunted him. As we talked about the ending of this relationship, he enlarged his description of their relationship and stated that he just could not stand being the "bad guy." This was the first time that he entertained the concept of being bad, selfish, and destructive. Although he is not able to harness his aggression, he has become able to contemplate, to reflect, to dream of himself being the "bad guy" and not need to foreclose that possibility. I hope these illustrations of moments of meeting in my work with Mr. X illustrate the process of transformation in analysis and the movement from the barrenness of being unable to imagine to a growing capacity for symbolic thought and a more creative unconscious and to becoming able to dream himself into existence.

Concluding Comments

This clinical illustration focuses on two interlocking dimensions in the process of transformation for a patient stuck in the deadened and deadening position of the contemporary patient. The first dimension is the inevitable and necessary impairment of the analyst's capacity to think, to enter states of reverie in which symmetrical, poetic, dreamlike, presentational processes can generate meaningful associations that can be used in the analytic dyad to generate subjective meaning. I think of this process as one of the difficulties in clinical work in which the analyst's capacity to contain the patient's experience breaks down, and both members of the analytic dyad become trapped in a concrete, paranoid state, overwhelmed by repetitive and meaningless experience. We might think of this inability to think as –K, and the analytic situation as being flooded with beta elements. The first task is for the analyst to recover or repair his capacity to be a container able to tolerate, accept, and affectively elaborate whatever thoughts occur, even those that reflect his/her own experiences of shame and guilt for being a failure as an analyst. Overcoming the guilt, shame, and hopelessness of being a failed analyst is necessary in order to begin to trust the process, oneself, and one's patient. This does not happen simply as an act of will or an asymmetrical cognitive exercise. Rather, this process of repairing the broken container (Newirth, 2018) is a complex procedural process in which we must be prepared to feel foolish and frequently fall on our face, as is necessary in learning to ride a bicycle, ski, or dance.

At the moment that I had the frightening association of being a prisoner in a cell, like in an old movie, crossing off the days of his/ my life, I initially wanted to escape from that image, as it suggested hopeless, helpless, suicidal depression. Deciding to tell Mr. X that association felt like it required a type of courage, perhaps because it was unclear which of us was actually the doomed prisoner, or perhaps both of us were. This represents a procedural experience, a 'now moment,' a difficult moment of recognition, which also reflects a movement from concrete thought processes of the paranoid schizoid position to a possible beginning process of symbolization and the generation of meaning, of becoming alive, of dreaming oneself into existence. I was quite surprised by Mr. X's response and our subsequent lively ability to enter into the transitional play around his earlier fascination with *Gunsmoke* and the Westerns of his childhood.

This moment, in which we entered into the world of playing with the Westerns, illustrates the second interlocking process, through which Mr. X was able to become enlivened and begin to generate meaning and a more active perspective on his life. Our conversations did more than simply articulate his unconscious fantasies, his unthought known. Through our playing together in this newly generated transitional space, he could become the cowboy that he had previously just been able to observe passively in a dissociated state. He could see how the underlying cowboy values had limited his life and his capacity for pleasure and, through the pleasure generated in our sessions, he was able to move into a new developmental position that we could understand as the depressive position or that of mentalization, being able to integrate the modes of psychic equivalence and the pretend mode. It is important to understand that this is a developmental process, a process of growth, of taking new, enlivened perspectives on one's life.

I hope that these moments from my work with Mr. X illustrate the transformation from states of unconscious deadness, from being stuck in a never-ending world of what is, into the possibility of being able to dream oneself into existence.

Notes

1 I see myself as working from a contemporary Kleinian perspective which is deeply influenced by relational psychoanalysis and developmental and linguistic perspectives.
2 If we think of the concept of the analytic third (Ogden, 1994; Benjamin, 2004), we may think of the collapse of the container contained relationship as merging into a one-dimensional analytic space of a concrete merger between patient and analyst.

References

Abend, S.M. (2007) Therapeutic Action in Modern Conflict Theory. *Psychoanalytic Quarterly*, 76: 1417–1442.

Abend, S.M. (2008) Unconscious Fantasy and Modern Conflict Theory. *Psychoanalytic Inquiry*, 28: 117–130.

Abend, S.M. (2009) Freud, Transference, and Therapeutic Action. *Psychoanalytic Quarterly*, 78: 871–892.

Ahbel-Rappe, K. (2009) "After a Long Pause": How to Read Dora as History. *Journal of the American Psychoanalytic Association*, 57: 595–629.

Appelbaum, D. (2010) On Learning to Inquire: Revisiting the Detailed Inquiry. *American Journal of Psychoanalysis*, 70: 78–85.

Arlow, J.A. & Brenner, C. (1988) The Future of Psychoanalysis. *Psychoanalytic Quarterly*, 57: 1–14.

Aron, L. (1989) Dreams, Narrative and the Psychoanalytic Method. *Contemporary Psychoanalysis*, 25: 108–126.

Aron, L. (1999) Clinical Choices and the Relational Matrix. *Psychoanalytic Dialogues*, 9: 1–29.

Aron, L. (2001) *A Meeting of Minds: Mutuality in Psychoanalysis*. New York: Routledge.

Asch, S.S. (1991) The Influencing Machine and the Mad Scientist: The Influence of Contemporary Culture on the Evolution of a Basic Delusion. *International Review of Psycho-Analysis*, 18: 185–193.

Axelrod, G. (Producer) & Frankenheimer, J. (Producer/Director). (1962) *The Manchurian Candidate* [Motion Picture]. Los Angeles, CA: United Artists.

Bass, A. (2015) The Dialogue of Unconsciouses, Mutual Analysis and the Uses of the Self in Contemporary Relational Psychoanalysis. *Psychoanalytic Dialogues*, 25: 2–17.

Beebe, B. (2005) Mother–Infant Research Informs Mother–Infant Treatment. *Psychoanalytic Study of the Child*, 60: 7–46.

Beebe, B., & Lachmann, F. (2020) Infant Research and Adult Treatment Revisited: Cocreating Self- and Interactive Regulation. *Psychoanalytic Psychology*, 37: 313–323.

Beebe, J. (1990) The Notorious Post War Psyche. *Journal of Popular Film and Television*, 18(1): 28–35.

Benjamin, J. (2004) Beyond Doer and Done To. *The Psychoanalytic Quarterly*, 73(1): 5–46.

Benjamin, J. (2009) A Relational Psychoanalysis Perspective on the Necessity of Acknowledging Failure in order to Restore the Facilitating and Containing Features of the Intersubjective Relationship (the Shared Third). *International Journal of Psychoanalysis*, 90: 441–450.

Biesen, S.C. (2014) Psychology in American Film Noir and Hitchcock's Gothic Thrillers. *Americana: The Journal of American Popular Culture,1900 to Present*, 13 (1). Retrieved from www.americanpopularcul ture.com/journal/articles/spring_2014/biesen.htm

Bion, W.R. (1959/2013) Attacks on Linking. *International Journal of Psychoanalysis*, 40: 308–315.

Bion, W.R. (1962) The Psycho-Analytic Study of Thinking. *International Journal of Psychoanalysis*, 43: 306–310.

Bion, W.R. (1965) *Transformations: Change from Learning to Growth*. London: Tavistock.

Bion, W.R. (1967) Notes on Memory and Desire. *The Psychoanalytic Forum*, 2: 272–273, 279–290.

Bion, W.R. (1970) Container and Contained Transformed. In *Attention and Interpretation: A Scientific Approach to Insight in Psycho-Analysis and Groups*. London: Tavistock, 106–124.

Bion, W.R. (2013) Attacks on Linking. *Psychoanalytic Quarterly*, 82: 285–300.

Blass, R.B., & Simon, B. (1994) The Value of the Historical Perspective to Contemporary Psychoanalysis: Freud's "Seduction Hypothesis." *International Journal of Psychoanalysis*, 75: 677–693.

Bloom, H. (1985) *Modern Critical Views: Sigmund Freud*. New York: Chelsea House.

Böhm, S., & Batta, A. (2010) Just Doing It: Enjoying Commodity Fetishism with Lacan. *Organization*, 17(3): 345–361.

B.P.C.S.G. (The Process of Change Study Group), Stern, D.N., Sander, L. W., Nahum, J.P., Harrison, A.M., Lyons-Ruth, K., Morgan, A.C., Bruschweiler-Stern, N., & Tronick, E.Z. (1998) Non-Interpretive

Mechanisms in Psychoanalytic Therapy. *International Journal of Psychoanalysis*, 79: 903–921.

Bowlby, J. (1999 [1969]) *Attachment and Loss: Volume 1, Attachment*, 2nd ed. New York: Basic Books.

Breuer, J., & Freud, S. (1893/1957) On The Psychical Mechanism of Hysterical Phenomena: Preliminary Communication from Studies on Hysteria. *The Standard Edition of the Complete Psychological Works of Sigmund Freud*, Vol. 2: 1–17.

Bromberg, P.M. (1980) Sullivan's Concept of Consensual Validation – Sullivan's Concept of Consensual Validation and the Therapeutic Action of Psychoanalysis. *Contemporary Psychoanalysis*, 16: 237–248.

Bromberg, P.M. (1993) Shadow and Substance: A Relational Perspective on Clinical Process. *Psychoanalytic Psychology*, 10: 147–168.

Bromberg, P.M. (1996) Standing in the Spaces: The Multiplicity of Self and the Psychoanalytic Relationship. *Contemporary Psychoanalysis*, 32: 509–535.

Brockman, R. (2010) Freud, Frankenstein, and the Art of Loss. *Psychoanalytic Review*, 97: 819–833.

Burke, W.F. (1992) Countertransference Disclosure and the Asymmetry/Mutuality Dilemma. *Psychoanalytic Dialogues*, 2: 241–271.

Cooper, M.C. (Producer/Director), Schoedsack, E.B. (Producer/Director), & Selznick, D.O. (Producer). (1933) *King Kong* [Motion Picture]. Los Angeles, CA: RKO Radio Pictures.

Crowley, R. (1978) Are Being Simply Human and Uniqueness Opposed? *Contemporary Psychoanalysis*, 14: 135–139.

Davies, J.M. (1994) Love in the Afternoon: A Relational Reconsideration of Desire and Dread in the Countertransference. *Psychoanalytic Dialogues*, 4: 153–170.

D'Costa, K. (2011) The American Fascination with Zombies. *Scientific American*, October 26. Retrieved from http://blogs.scientificamerican.com/anthropology-in-practice/the-american-fascination-with-zombies

Denby, D. (2013) Life and Undeath: World War Z. *The New Yorker*, July 1. Retrieved from www.newyorker.com/magazine/2013/07/01/life-and-undeath

Dor, J. (1997) *The Clinical Lacan*. Northvale, NJ: Jason Aronson.

Ferenczi, S. (1988) Confusion of Tongues between Adults and the Child: The Language of Tenderness and of Passion. *Contemporary Psychoanalysis*, 24(2): 196–206.

Ferro, A. (2006) Clinical Implications of Bion's Thought. *International Journal of Psychoanalysis*, 87(4): 989–1003.

Ferro, A. (2009) Transformations in Dreaming and Characters in the Psychoanalytic Field. *International Journal of Psychoanalysis*, 90(2): 209–230.

Ferro, A. (2012) Creativity in the Consulting Room: Factors of Fertility and Infertility. *Psychoanalytic Inquiry*, 32(3): 257–274.

Fonagy, P. (1995) Playing with Reality: The Development of Psychic Reality and its Malfunction in Borderline Personalities. *International Journal of Psychoanalysis*, 76: 39–44.

Fonagy, P. (2008) A Genuinely Developmental Theory of Sexual Enjoyment and Its Implications for Psychoanalytic Technique. *Journal of the American Psychoanalytic Association*, 56: 11–36.

Fonagy, P. (2014) *Attachment Theory and Psychoanalysis: The Need for a New Integration?*Anna Freud Center Video Collection1:1.

Fonagy, P., & Target, M. (2007) Playing with Reality: IV. A Theory of External Reality Rooted in Intersubjectivity. *International Journal of Psychoanalysis*, 88(4): 917–937.

Freud, S. (1896a) *Further Remarks on the Neuro-Psychoses of Defence*. S. E., Vol. III: 157–185.

Freud, S. (1896b) *The Aetiology of Hysteria*. S.E., Vol. III.

Freud, S. (1900) *The Interpretation of Dreams*. S.E., Vol. IV.

Freud, S. (1901) *The Psychopathology of Everyday Life: Forgetting, Slips of the Tongue, Bungled Actions, Superstitions and Errors*. S.E., Vol. VI: vii–296.

Freud, S. (1905) *Fragment of an Analysis of a Case of Hysteria in Three Essays on Sexuality and Other Works*. S.E., Vol. VII: 1–122.

Freud, S. (1909) *Notes Upon a Case of Obsessional Neurosis in Two Case Histories ("Little Hans" and the "Rat Man")*. S.E., Vol. X: 151–318.

Freud, S. (1915a) *Repression*. S.E., Vol. XIV: 141–158.

Freud, S. (1915b) *The Unconscious*. S.E., Vol. XIV: 159–215.

Freud, S. (1917) *A Metapsychological Supplement to the Theory of Dreams. S.E.*, Vol. 14: 217–235.

Freud, S. (1920) *Beyond the Pleasure Principle. S.E.*, Vol. IV: 1–64.

Freud, S. (1925) *An Autobiographical Study. S.E.*, Vol. XX.

Freud, S. (1937) *Constructions in Analysis. S.E.*, Vol. XXIII: 255–270.

Fromm, E. (1951) *The Forgotten Language*. New York: Rhinehard.

Fromm, E. (1994) *Escape from Freedom*. New York: Macmillan.

Gabbard, G.O., & Gabbard, K. (1999) *Psychiatry and the Cinema*, 2nd ed. Washington, DC: American Psychiatric Press.

Ginot, E. (2009) The Empathic Power of Enactments: The Link between Neuropsychological Processes and an Expanded Definition of Empathy. *Psychoanalytic Psychology*, 36(3): 290–309.

Green, A. (1993) The Dead Mother [Die tote Mutter]. *Psyche*, 47(3): 205–240.

Green, M.R. (1964) *Interpersonal Psychoanalysis: The Selected Papers of Clara M. Thompson*. New York: Basic Books.

Greenberg, J., & Mitchell, S.A. (1983) *Object Relations in Psychoanalytic Theory.* Cambridge, MA: Harvard University Press.

Grosskurth, P. (1986) *Melanie Klein.* New York: Knopf.

Grotstein, J. (1995) Orphans of the Real I. *Bulletin of the Menninger Clinic,* 59(3): 287–311.

Hardman, K. (Producer), Streiner, R. (Producer), & Romero, G.A. (Director). (1968) *Night of the Living Dead* [Motion Picture]. Los Angeles, CA: Walter Reade Organization.

Havens, L.L. (1976) *Participant Observation.* New York: J. Aronson.

Hirsch, I. (1992) Extending Sullivan's Interpersonalism. *Contemporary Psychoanalysis,* 28: 732–747.

Hitchcock, A. (Producer/Director). (1946) *Notorious* [Motion Picture]. Los Angeles, CA: RKO Radio Pictures.

Hitchcock, A. (Producer/Director). (1960) *Psycho* [Motion Picture]. Los Angeles, CA: Paramount Pictures.

Jagger, M., & Richards, K. (1965) *(I Can't Get No) Satisfaction.* Recorded by The Rolling Stones.

Joseph, B. (1985) Transference: The Total Situation. *International Journal of Psychoanalysis,* 66: 447–454.

Khan, M.M. (1974) *The Privacy of the Self.* New York: Routledge.

Khan, M.M. (2019) *Alienation in Perversions.* New York: Routledge.

Klein, E. (2022) I Didn't Want It to Be True, but the Medium Really Is the Message. *New York Times,* August 7.

Klein, M. (1931) A Contribution to the Theory of Intellectual Inhibition. *International Journal of Psychoanalysis,* 12: 206–218.

Klein, M. (1975) *Envy and Gratitude and Other Works 1946–1963.* Ed. M. Masud & R. Khan, The International Psycho-Analytic Library, Vol. 104. London: Hogarth Press and Institute of Psycho-Analysis, 1–346.

Kohut, H. (1971) *The Analysis of the Self: A Systematic Approach to the Psychoanalytic Treatment of Narcissistic Personality Disorders.* Chicago, IL: University of Chicago Press.

Kohut, H. (1979) The Two Analyses of Mr Z. *International Journal of Psychoanalysis,* 60: 3–27.

Kohut, H. (1984) *How Does Analysis Cure?* Chicago, IL: University of Chicago Press.

Lacan, J. (1977) *The Four Fundamental Concepts of Psychoanalysis.* Ed. J.-A. Miller. Trans. A. Sheridan. New York: W.W. Norton.

Lacan, J. (2006) *Écrits: The First Complete Edition in English.* Trans. B. Fink. New York: W.W. Norton.

Lakoff, G., & Johnson, M. (1999) *Philosophy in the Flesh: The Embodied Mind and Its Challenge to Western Thought.* New York: Basic Books.

Langer, S. (1942) *Philosophy in a New Key*. Cambridge, MA: Harvard University Press.

Lema, A. (2012) A Perfectly Modern Frankenstein: Almodovar's The Skin I Live In. *International Journal of Psychoanalysis*, 93: 1291–1299.

Levenson, E.A. (1981) Facts or Fantasies: On the Nature of Psychoanalytic Data. *Contemporary Psychoanalysis*, 17: 486–500.

Levenson, E.A. (1988) The Pursuit of the Particular – On the Psychoanalytic Inquiry. *Contemporary Psychoanalysis*, 24: 1–16.

Levenson, E.A. (2003) On Seeing What Is Said: Visual Aids to the Psychoanalytic Process. *Contemporary Psychoanalysis*, 39: 233–249.

Levenson, E.A. (2005) *The Fallacy of Understanding*. Hillsdale, NJ: Analytic Press.

Lewis, M. (2011) *The Big Short: Inside the Doomsday Machine*. New York: Norton.

Mancia, M. (2006) Implicit Memory and Early Unrepressed Unconscious: Their Role in the Therapeutic Process (How the Neurosciences Can Contribute to Psychoanalysis). *International Journal of Psychoanalysis*, 87: 83–103.

Matte Blanco, I. (1975) *The Unconscious as Infinite Sets: An Essay in Bi-logic*. London: Gerald Duckworth (republished by Karnac, 1998).

Matte Blanco, I. (1981) Reflecting with Bion. In J.S. Grostein (ed.), *Do I Dare Disturb the Universe: A Memorial to WR Bion*. London: Karnac, 489–528.

Matte Blanco, I. (1988) *Thinking, Feeling and Being: Clinical Reflections on the Fundamental Antinomy of the Human Being and World*. London: Routledge.

Mitchell, S.A. (1990) The Analyst's Knowledge and Authority. *Psychoanalytic Quarterly*, 67: 1–31.

Mitchell, S.A. (1991) Wishes, Needs and Interpersonal Negotiation. *Psychoanalytic Inquiry*, 11: 147–170.

Monroe, R.L. (1955) *Schools of Psychoanalytic Thought*. New York: Dryden Press.

Newirth, J. (2003) *Between Emotion and Cognition: The Generative Unconscious*. New York: Other Press.

Newirth, J. (2015) Psychoanalysis' Past, Present, and Future: Sherlock Holmes, Sir Lancelot, and the Wizard of Oz. *Psychoanalytic Psychology*, 32: 307–320.

Newirth, J. (2018) *From Sign to Symbol: Transformational Processes in Psychoanalysis, Psychotherapy and Psychology*. New York: Lexington Books.

Ogden, T.H. (1992) The Dialectically Constituted/Decentred Subject of Psychoanalysis. II. The Contributions of Klein and Winnicott. *International Journal of Psychoanalysis*, 73: 613–626.

Ogden, T.H. (1994) The Analytic Third: Working with Intersubjective Clinical Facts. *International Journal of Psychoanalysis*, 75: 3–19.

Ogden, T.H. (1995) Analysing Forms of Aliveness and Deadness of the Transference-Countertransference. *International Journal of Psychoanalysis*, 76: 695–709.

Ogden, T.H. (2004) The Art of Psychoanalysis: Dreaming Undreamt Dreams and Interrupted Cries. *International Journal of Psychoanalysis*, 85: 857–878.

Ogden, T.H. (2007) On Talking-as-Dreaming. *International Journal of Psychoanalysis*, 88: 575–589.

Ogden, T.H. (2010) On Three Forms of Thinking: Magical Thinking, Dream Thinking, and Transformative Thinking. *Psychoanalytic Quarterly*, 79: 317–347.

Perry, H.S. (1982) *Psychiatrist of America: The Life of Henry Stack Sullivan*. New York: Belknap Press.

Piaget, J. (1973) The Affective Unconscious and the Cognitive Unconscious. *Journal of the American Psychoanalytic Association*, 21: 249–261.

Racker, H. (1982) *Transference and Countertransference*. New York: Routledge.

Rayner, E. (1995) *Unconscious Logic: An Introduction to Matte Blanco's Bi-logic and Its Uses*. London: Routledge.

Reik, T. (1959) New Ways in Psychoanalytic Technique. *Psychoanalytic Review*, 46: 51–64.

Schafer, R. (1976) *A New Language for Psychoanalysis*. New Haven, CT: Yale University Press.

Schoenhals, H. (1995) Triangular Space and the Development of a Working Model in the Analysis. *International Journal of Psychoanalysis*, 76: 103–113.

Schore, A.N. (2011) The Right Brain Implicit Self Lies at the Core of Psychoanalysis. *Psychoanalytic Dialogues*, 21: 75–100.

Searles, H. (1979) *Countertransference and Related Subjects*. New York: International Universities Press.

Segal, H. (1978) On Symbolism. *International Journal of Psychoanalysis*, 59: 315–319.

Selznick, D.O., & Hitchcock, A. (1945) *Spellbound* [Motion Picture]. Los Angeles, CA: United Artists

Shaviro, S. (2002) Capitalist Monsters. *Historical Materialism*, 10: 281–290. http://dx.doi.org/10.1163/15692060260474486

Singer, E. (1971) The Patient Aids the Analyst: Some Clinical and Theoretical Observations. In B. Landis & E.S. Tauber (eds.), *In the Name of Life. Essays in Honor of Erich Fromm.* New York: Holt, Rinehart & Winston, 56–68.

Stein, M. (2011) A Culture of Mania: A Psychoanalytic View of the Incubation of the 2008 Credit Crisis. *Organization*, 18: 173–186. http://dx.doi.org/10.1177/1350508410390071

Stern, D.B. (2013) Field Theory in Psychoanalysis, Part 2: Bionian Field Theory and Contemporary Interpersonal/Relational Psychoanalysis. *Psychoanalytic Dialogues*, 23: 630–645.

Stern, D.B. (2019) Unformulated Experience and the Relational Turn. *Psychoanalytic Inquiry*, 39: 127–135.

Stern, D.N. (1985) *The Interpersonal World of the Human Infant.* New York: Basic Books.

Stern, D.N. (1992) The "Pre-Narrative Envelope": An Alternative View of "Unconscious Phantasy" in Infancy. *Bulletin of the Anna Freud Centre*, 15: 291–318.

Sullivan, H.S. (1970) *The Psychiatric Interview.* New York: Norton

Sullivan, H.S. (2013). *The Interpersonal Theory of Psychiatry.* New York: Routledge.

Symington, N. (1983) The Analyst's Act of Freedom as Agent of Therapeutic Change. *International Review of Psychoanalysis*, 10: 283–291.

Symington, N. (2007) A Technique for the Creation of Mind. *The International Journal of Psychoanalysis*, 88: 1409–1422.

Szasz, T. (2010) *The Myth of Mental Illness.* New York: Harper Collins.

Whale, J. (1931). *Frankenstein.* Universal Pictures.

Weinberger, J., & Stoycheva, V. (2021) *The Unconscious: Theory, Research, and Clinical Implications.* New York: Guilford Press.

Winnicott, D.W. (1971) *Playing and Reality.* New York: Tavistock.

Winnicott, D.W. (1974) Fear of Breakdown. *International Review of Psychoanalysis*, 1: 103–107.

Winnicott, D.W. (1975) *Through Paediatrics to Psycho-Analysis.* London: Hogarth Press and Institute of Psycho-Analysis.

Winnicott, D., Winnicott, C., Shepherd, R., & Davis, M. (1989) *Psycho-Analytic Explorations.* New York: Routledge.

Wolf, N.S., Gales, M.E., Shane, E., & Shane, M. (2001) The Developmental Trajectory from Amodal Perception to Empathy and Communication: The Role of Mirror Neurons in this Process. *Psychoanalytic Inquiry*, 21: 94–112.

Index

9780367525170